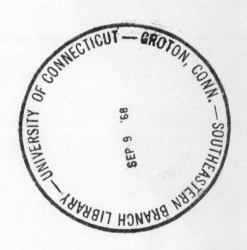

THE SUMMIT CONFERENCES, 1919–1960

THE
SUMMIT
CONFERENCES
1919-1960

By Keith Eubank

UNIVERSITY OF OKLAHOMA PRESS : NORMAN

BY KEITH EUBANK

Paul Cambon: Master Diplomatist (Norman, 1960)

Munich (Norman, 1963)

The Summit Conferences, 1919–1960 (Norman, 1966)

LIBRARY OF CONGRESS CATALOG CARD NUMBER: 66–22711

TO MARILYN'S FATHER AND MOTHER,
J. WARREN CLIMENSON AND JEANETTE M. CLIMENSON

Preface

IN AN AGE of specialization when there has been little demand for amateurs, they have shouldered the professionals aside in one field of diplomacy: the summit conference. There politicians have assumed the roles once assigned to professional diplomats.

With either a few days' briefing or perhaps none at all, these neophyte diplomats met in summit conferences where they grappled with weighty international problems. Although these men lacked training, none of them hesitated to wrestle with problems involving frontiers, populations, disputed territories, or financial crises affecting millions of the living and unborn.

At home the public too often expected these men to produce instant solutions to international ills. The same public, however, would never have demanded expert performances from novices of medicine, law, education, or any other specialized field of human endeavor.

Because the secrecy and disappointing results of these conferences have bred a host of myths, and because they have had an influence on recent history, they warrant study. The story of the summit conference, the value of its method of negotiation, and its weaknesses are the substance of this book.

I am deeply grateful to everyone who has helped me in this venture. My wife, Marilyn Climenson Eubank, always encouraged and aided me in my labors. Carol Oakey typed much of the manuscript and assisted in the research and writing. Professor Richard Kottman, a former colleague at North Texas State University, read the manuscript, gave it a searching review, and made many constructive suggestions. Members of my graduate seminar at North Texas State University made substantial contributions by their study of many facets of summit conference history. I am especially indebted to the staffs of the North Texas State University Library and the Paul Klapper Library of Queens College. Research grants from the Faculty Research fund of North Texas State University helped finance my research.

KEITH EUBANK

Melville, New York
October 4, 1966

Contents

	Preface	*vii*
1.	One Morning in May	3
2.	Paris, 1919	9
3.	The Czechoslovak Crisis	32
4.	Munich, 1938	41
5.	In Search of a Conference	50
6.	Teheran, 1943	58
7.	Yalta, 1945	79
8.	Between War and Peace	106
9.	Potsdam, 1945	114
10.	A Cold War Summit?	135
11.	Geneva, 1955	144
12.	A Conference for Khrushchev	160

13. The U–2   175
14. Paris Again, 1960   183
15. A Verdict   194
     Bibliography   210
     Index   217

Illustrations

The Big Four at Paris, 1919   *facing page* 52
Munich and "Appeasement," 1938   53
Teheran, 1943—The Price of Soviet Co-operation   68
Yalta, 1945—The Terms of Teheran Are Reinforced   69
Potsdam, 1945—The Fate of Eastern Europe Is Sealed   148
Geneva, 1955—Another Disappointing Summit Conference   149
Paris, 1960—Khrushchev Shatters the Hopes
    of the Free World   164
Premier Khrushchev during the Dark Hours of May 17, 1960   165

THE SUMMIT CONFERENCES, 1919–1960

One Morning in May

FOUR MEN sat in a delightful eighteenth-century room within the Elysée Palace. Outside along the boulevards spring had come to Paris, but not one of the four was concerned with the weather on May 16, 1960. A bald Ukrainian peasant, Nikita S. Khrushchev, premier of the Soviet Union, ordered apologies and promises of future good behavior from the President of the United States, Dwight D. Eisenhower. The former general was tense, his face set and white. Harold Macmillan, the British prime minister, endured the tirade, grieving over his vanished hope for a useful meeting. Another observer was hawk-nosed Charles de Gaulle, former general and president of the Fifth French Republic. He had insisted that the meeting be held in Paris at his convenience for reasons of national prestige.

Khrushchev required an apology from President Eisenhower for the flight of a United States plane across the Soviet Union. The plane had not strayed across the Russian frontiers because the pilot had forgotten the art of navigation. Under orders from the Central Intelligence Agency, the pilot had deliberately penetrated the closely guarded Russian frontier a few days earlier to photograph strategic installations.

To satisfy Khrushchev, those responsible must be punished. Eisenhower must issue a formal renunciation of this "aggressive" action. Khrushchev knew the purpose of the flight because Soviet rocket batteries had brought the plane down. Soviet peasants had captured the pilot, Francis Gary Powers, who had neglected to blow up himself and his plane as his superiors had planned.

Newspapermen had flocked to Paris from all over the world to report on the deliberations of this quartet. Months had been spent in diplomatic sparring over the summoning of this meeting, which the press called a "summit conference." The four heads of government were expected to settle the ills of the world while shut off from outside distractions. But a lonely parachutist descending out of the Russian skies spoiled the plans for a genteel conference about world affairs. Now the Soviet premier damned the United States Air Force, American espionage, and violations of the Russian frontiers.

After two days of tragicomedy, the conference collapsed without Khrushchev receiving satisfaction. Nothing constructive had been accomplished. But Powers, the unlucky pilot, had helped end an epoch in the history of diplomacy when chiefs of state and heads of government had negotiated directly over war and peace. Never again would statesmen approach a summit conference without pondering the tale of Powers and that morning in May.

From 1919–60, on seven occasions, heads of government gathered to consider the world's problems in meetings that could be called "summit conferences." They were by-products of the twentieth-century world wars. The title was coined by

4

the newspapermen who had derived it from Sir Winston Churchill's speech in 1953.

> I believe that a conference on the highest level should take
> place between the leading powers without delay. . . . If there is
> not at the summit of the nations the will to win the greatest prize
> and the greatest honor ever offered to mankind, doom-laden
> responsibility will fall upon those who now possess the power
> to decide.[1]

In a world surfeited with wars and crises, Sir Winston's idea
seemed a possible solution. The heads of government of the great
powers would meet privately to consider man-to-man the awful
problems of international affairs. Diplomats would be excluded
except to interpret or to advise in case of emergency. Emer-
gencies would arise when a tribe, a mountain, or a river could
not be located.

Instead of striped-pants diplomats, elected politicians
would negotiate. Neither legal technicalities nor protocol would
prevent them from reaching a decision. Being practical men,
they would sweep towards their objective and reach it. More
than the diplomats, they would have the true interests of mankind as their guide. Because of their power, the members of the
summit conference could act swiftly to solve the world's ills.
They could determine policy and immediately put it into action
—a virtue in the time of nuclear warfare. Nothing would hamper
their quest because they had the authority, the will, and the
desire to reach their goal. From their deliberations would come
agreements to change the course of history for the benefit of
mankind.

The summit conference can be defined as chiefs of state or
heads of government meeting privately to discuss and to settle
world problems. The summit conference has become different
by virtue of the attendance and active participation of the heads

[1] *Parliamentary Debates, House of Commons,* Fifth Series, Vol. 515, cols.
883–98.

of government of the great powers. In the current meaning, the summit conference is more than a pair talking. A conference of two chiefs of state or heads of government has not been rare in history, for monarchs often visited for the purpose of negotiating. But a summit conference is not two leaders talking quietly but three, four, or more acting as the sole negotiators for their nations with the foreign ministers relegated to subsidiary roles.

Since 1919 seven international conferences were significant for their historical importance and the notoriety of those present. The conferences were unique because chiefs of state and heads of government conferred over weighty matters. The foreign ministers and professional diplomats had only minor roles. The seven conferences were not official visits of state to promote friendly relations. These were summit conferences because the final decision belonged to the assembled chiefs of state and heads of government.

In the past, meetings of monarchs had not been unusual. Medieval diplomacy was often conducted by monarchs face-to-face without publicity or reporters present. The chancellors stood by to record the agreements on suitable parchment with impressive seals attached. These monarchs functioned as chiefs of state and heads of government, thus they could take the necessary steps in implementing the policy. Only the chancellor might bring up some technicality. Even the dukes and barons could be kept away.

The press of work, the growing complexities of government, and the need of a resident agent forced the monarchs to turn the job of diplomacy over to professionals. Thus began the classical age of diplomacy. Armed with his instructions, the diplomat set forth into a strange land to represent his sovereign. The slowness of travel and equally slow communications gave him importance and independence. Because of the separation from his master, the diplomat could often conduct negotiations according to his inclinations, subject only to the instructions.

6

Treaties could also be negotiated by the professional, including agreements ending wars.

But an exception was the Congress of Vienna, called in 1814 to deal with the treaties and problems growing out of the Napoleonic conflict. Czar Alexander I of Russia upset tradition by appearing in person to take an active role in negotiations. He was his own foreign minister, but also he was constitutionally the head of the government and the chief of state. Although the Austrian emperor and the Prussian king were present, neither took so active a part in the conference as did Alexander. Klemens von Metternich, by then chancellor of Austria, and Alexander negotiated, but they were the only heads of government actively participating.

In 1878, Benjamin Disraeli, British prime minister, and Otto von Bismarck, the German chancellor, negotiated in the Congress of Berlin. They were the only heads of government to take part because professional diplomats were still the rule.

Swifter communications and the revolution in transportation altered diplomacy. No longer was the diplomat's isolation so complete because the foreign minister could more easily direct his negotiations. World War I required co-ordination of diplomacy with the direction of global war. The politician who could cut through red tape and achieve results received national support and could speak with greater mandate from the nation. The length of the conflict increased the demand for an end to the blood bath. Because the Allied Powers so long resisted the appointment of an Allied commander-in-chief or Allied joint chiefs of staff, the political leaders were tempted to bypass their diplomats in co-ordinating the war effort. Once the heads of government began taking a more direct role in treating with other premiers and prime ministers, regular summit conferences were inevitable.

The world conflict of 1914–18 brought to power leaders who distrusted the practices of professional diplomats. To these ambitious politicians, negotiations carried on by professional dip-

7

lomats appeared time consuming, consecrated to senseless protocol. The diplomats seemed unable to settle affairs as swiftly and efficiently as the new leaders who spoke for the masses. When democracy seemed everywhere victorious, professional diplomats were leftovers from a more aristocratic age. Could not the politician's skill replace the experience and training of a career diplomat? The heads of the Allied governments were the first to test this proposition which was fundamental to any summit conference. Without training and with slight experience, the heads of government were better negotiators than the professionals.

In 1919 came the first of seven summit conferences when amateurs replaced the professionals. They continued until one May morning when an American pilot, ejected from his falling plane, wrecked a summit conference. All of these conferences have been disputed. All affected modern history.

2

Paris, 1919

L EADERS of the Allied nations blamed secret diplomacy for
World War I. Professional diplomats had secretly constructed
entangling alliances which many thought had caused the war.
Allied politicians were convinced that in the future they must
control diplomacy to insure peace. The professionals could not
be trusted.

During the war, elected heads of government took on tasks
which had formerly been allotted to professional diplomats. Because of their distrust for the professional diplomats and the
need for speed, the heads of governments often bypassed their
foreign offices. David Lloyd George, the British prime minister,
created his own private foreign office next to No. 10 Downing
Street, ignoring Lord Balfour, the foreign secretary. President

Woodrow Wilson selected Colonel Edward House, a Texas politician, as his private emissary, communicating through him with other Allied governments. Wilson deliberately failed to inform Secretary of State Robert Lansing.

When the terrible struggle ended, popularly elected heads of government could not remain absent from the Paris Peace Conference. Wilson's decision to attend the conference as the chief of the American delegation signified a revolution in United States diplomacy. For the first time a President would leave the country and personally negotiate. The task would not be delegated to Secretary Lansing or a professional diplomat. The presence of the President of the United States of America altered the spirit of the peace conference. Wilson had made a summit conference inevitable.

Although Premier Georges Clemenceau of France, Prime Minister Lloyd George of Great Britain, and Premier Vittorio Orlando of Italy came to Paris, there was no conscious plan to have a summit conference. Yet one developed without planning. The wars, the ideas, and personalities of the Allied leaders produced the summit conference.

In 1916 and 1917 there had been Allied meetings with the premiers present and taking leading roles. This group, known as the Inter-Allied Committee, became the Supreme War Council in 1917 when military leaders were added. In 1918, Colonel House sat on the council as President Woodrow Wilson's personal representative. In the last months of the war, this council became the central directing agency for the Allied forces. When Wilson came to Paris, he took his place on this council.

On January 12, 1919, the Supreme War Council held the first meeting of the preliminary peace conference. After Marshal Ferdinand Foch, Allied commander-in-chief, reported on the German execution of the armistice terms, he and other military leaders withdrew. The Supreme War Council became the Council of Ten and began consideration of the peace conference. The heads of government and the foreign ministers of the United

States, France, Great Britain, Italy, and Japan composed the Council of Ten. On January 13, at Wilson's suggestion, they agreed to meet together to "find out their own minds before they entered into the process of the peace conference."[1] The other delegates would assemble for a plenary session, but nothing significant would be done. The council had no intention of allowing a general debate in the plenary session. The delegates of the five powers would iron out their differences and decide what was ready for solution.[2]

For the next two months the Council of Ten dominated the Paris Peace Conference. Gradually the Council of Ten increased in size until, by March 21, fifty-three members were present, including seventeen secretaries. Amid so many it became impossible to avoid news leakage to the press. Lloyd George complained that details of a previous meeting on the Polish problem had been revealed to Paris newspapers. Tighter security was imperative.

Not only was there unwanted publicity, but the peace conference was being criticized for its lack of results. For the German treaty the conference had agreed on a division of colonies and some military terms. A draft of the Covenant of the League of Nations had been completed. Wilson's return to the United States in February produced more delay. By the time he returned in March, there was a growing desire to speed up the conference procedure. Because so large a group made effective negotiations almost impossible, the obvious solution seemed to be smaller meetings of a more private nature.

Wilson had contemplated such a procedure for some time because he considered scores of delegates quarreling over a treaty nothing but a waste of time. A small group could draft proposals for submission to the full conference. He wanted a group similar to the Senate Foreign Relations Committee with

[1] *Foreign Relations of the United States* (hereafter cited as *FRUS*), *Paris Peace Conference, 1919*, III, 537.
[2] *Ibid.*, 423, 444–47.

greater secrecy surrounding its meetings. Only the discussions in full conference would be open to the public.[3]

Already there had been private meetings to speed up the conference. Wilson had conferred with David Lloyd George, Georges Clemenceau, the French premier, and Premier Vittorio Orlando of Italy. On March 24, Wilson proposed that the four meet privately at his apartment because of public impatience over the delay in the treaty. They could discuss the most difficult and urgent problems. Once these were settled, the rest could be decided quickly. Leaks to the newspapers could be stopped. The trio accepted Wilson's suggestion.[4] Thereafter they usually met at 11:00 A.M. and at 4:00 P.M. in Wilson's apartment in the *place des États-Unis*. Sometimes they assembled in Lloyd George's residence, occasionally in Clemenceau's office, and very rarely in the Ministry of Foreign Affairs.

The council was informal in its operations. Anyone could introduce subjects for discussion; there does not seem to have been any formal agenda. In practice there was no chairman. The members took up whatever troubled their spirits or whatever had been forwarded to them for action. Committees presented reports, and the council often used these reports as the basis for discussions. The council functioned best when its discussions were based on a committee report because without such a base the discussion strayed off into every direction. Decisions were unanimous, and there were no motions. However, one member might reserve his approval until after consultation with his experts.

Whenever their opinions were needed, the experts were summoned before the council. After making their report, they

[3] Herbert Hoover, *The Ordeal of Woodrow Wilson*, 195; Arthur Walworth, *Woodrow Wilson: World Prophet*, II, 241; Robert Lansing, *The Big Four and Others of the Peace Conference*, 85–86.

[4] Paul Mantoux, *Les délibérations du conseil des quatre (24 mars–28 juin, 1919)*, I, 13–17; Walworth, *Woodrow Wilson*, II, 226–27, 282–88. Clemenceau, Lloyd George, and Wilson had met unofficially before March 24.

usually withdrew, leaving the council to argue out the problem. Sometimes the experts' presence only prolonged the discussions.

The Council of Four often referred subjects to the foreign ministers for action or study. Occasionally they were summoned for their opinions, but there was no regular consultation between the foreign ministers and the Council of Four.

Except for the four heads of government, only Paul Mantoux, the official interpreter, was present during the first meetings. Because the four politicians were often in doubt over what they had agreed upon, in mid-April Maurice Hankey was appointed secretary. A former secretary of the Committee of Imperial Defense, Hankey brought needed efficiency into the council's operations. Hankey informed the council of matters needing action, took down minutes of the meetings, kept their files in order, and functioned as a liaison with the committees of experts.

The secrecy of the council meetings was almost too perfect. The delegations and even the foreign ministers were forced to swap gossip and rumor for news. Wilson at last relented and dictated press releases to Ray Stannard Baker, his press secretary. Thus the President's views became the official version of the daily work of the Council of Four which the newspapers were permitted to publish.

When the conference ended and the Germans had signed the treaty, Hankey asked for a decision on the disposition of the minutes because he had received requests for copies. Immediately the council rejected publication. Wilson declared that because these were purely private conversations the minutes were private records; they were private property. The council could pass on the minutes to a trusted confidant but not to their successors in office. Clemenceau and Lloyd George refused to abide by this restriction. Their successors must be informed about the minutes.[5] The secrecy of these minutes ham-

[5] Lansing, *The Big Four and Others*, 65–66; *FRUS*, VI, 752–55; Mantoux, *Les délibérations*, I, 7; ibid., II, 563–66; Ray Stannard Baker, *Woodrow Wilson*

pered the writing of the history of the peace conference and remained unpublished until 1946.

The four leaders sat in comfortable chairs. There was only one table which Mantoux used, but Hankey had to use his lap for a desk as he recorded the minutes of the meeting. When maps were needed, they were spread on the floor, and the distinguished delegates crawled about on all fours.

The quartet was a mixture of ideas, philosophies, and experiences. Tough, old Clemenceau was at the peak of his career. As a Paris city official, he had watched with sorrow the defeat of France in 1870 and the Paris Commune in 1871. As a newspaper editor and as a deputy, Clemenceau became a power in the politics of the Third Republic. He was so hated and feared that in the worst hours of the war French politicians dreaded turning to Clemenceau when he alone could lead the nation. As the host to the peace conference, he presided in the plenary meetings and the Council of Ten. Now he would guarantee that France would be forever secure against German aggression.

Clemenceau believed that his colleagues regarded the future too optimistically and warned them that Germany would sign the treaty with a firm intention not to execute it. Germany would overwhelm them with notes and make the treaty a "perpetual controversy." By then the American troops would be far away.[6]

David Lloyd George was at the height of his powers. The nimble-minded Welshman had used the war to force Herbert Asquith out as prime minister. He had arrived at the peace conference after winning a general election. In the heat of the campaign some of his political associates advocated hanging Kaiser Wilhelm II and squeezing enormous reparations out of Germany. Lloyd George never corrected these exaggerated statements although his speeches were moderate in tone. Never-

---

and World Settlement; Written from his Unpublished and Personal Material, I, 131–34, 154.
    [6] *FRUS,* V, 637; Mantoux, *Les délibérations,* II, 239.

theless, Lloyd George was in debt to these extremists because they provided him with the necessary majority in the House of Commons. He would not disown them.

Seldom was Lloyd George without an opinion. He was more of a politician than either Wilson or Clemenceau, and he was the best negotiator. He was the least obstinate and sought in every way to reach a settlement.

Vittorio Orlando said little until he put forward the Italian claims. He had little influence on the German treaty until his insistence on discussing the Italian claims paralyzed the council's work. The fact that he was short and rotund, with a heavy white mustache, white hair, and dimpled smile, gave him a friendly air. His inability to speak English hampered him in the negotiations. Because Clemenceau spoke English, some of the meetings were conducted in English, much to the disadvantage of Orlando.

Woodrow Wilson was a former professor of government, president of Princeton University, and governor of New Jersey. His Scotch-Presbyterian heritage implanted in him a belief in the existence of right and wrong. He believed sincerely that he had come to the Old World bringing the newfound wisdom of the United States. Often he could not refrain from delivering a short sermon on the principles of justice that should govern the world henceforth. Neither Lloyd George nor Clemenceau really wanted him at the conference.

Wilson expressed less dissatisfaction with the German treaty than did either Clemenceau or Lloyd George. He feared that the Germans might not sign, but once they did so, he believed they would fulfill the terms. Plans to insure fulfillment were anathema to him. Only with reluctance was he brought to accept trials for war criminals. Once the treaty had been completed, he was loath to change it because he held it to be a just treaty. The Germans were receiving what was their rightful punishment.

Wilson, not Clemenceau, was the dominant figure of the

Council of Four. When he was willing to do battle he could obtain his ends. If he could enlist Lloyd George, Clemenceau usually gave way after prolonged oratory. One of Wilson's few defeats was the reparations question, which he could have won if he had fought as bitterly as he did on other questions.

The records of the Council of Four reveal only confusion in the discussion of the reparations owed by Germany. When the question came before the council, the experts were divided. The council could not proceed, but instead had to perform the experts' task. None of the quartet really understood the problems involved in reparations. Fourteen men quickly made the meetings sound like an economic Alice in Wonderland. No one questioned the justice of reparations. They could not agree on the sum to be demanded of Germany. To require four men, without any training in economics, surrounded by quarreling experts, to quickly judge the best course was asking much of human abilities.

The French proposed a total of $50,000,000,000, which Wilson insisted was the national capitalization of France in 1908. Germany could never pay this amount. Lloyd George would accept $25,000,000 until his own delegation disputed this sum among themselves. Clemenceau suggested that Germany's total liability be determined by an arbitration commission. The council need only "proclaim the principle of payment of war damages . . . without indicating a total obligatory sum." Wilson argued for a fixed sum in the treaty.[7]

On March 28, Lloyd George and Orlando took their stand in favor of omitting a fixed sum in the treaty terms. Lloyd George argued against continued discussion over the sum of reparations because whatever sum upon which they agreed the public and parliament would judge too small. He dreaded the strain on relations between the powers over this question.

Wilson made only a mild objection. He appeared unwilling to fight this issue. The problem did not seem to him as important

[7] *Ibid.*, I, 29–30.

as other matters which were then before the council, particularly the Rhineland and Saar questions. Isolated on this question, Wilson needed support on other problems. The treaty would require an unspecified sum of reparations.

Wilson could have undermined the opposition by proposing full or partial cancellation of inter-Allied war debts in return for a moderate reparations sum. The President and his advisers refused. If they had attempted such an arrangement, Congress would have demolished it. Regardless of the total reparations demanded of Germany, the Allies must pay their debts to the United States.[8]

Flu forced Wilson to absent himself from the turmoil, leaving as his substitute Colonel Edward M. House, who was improperly briefed. The Colonel did not understand the ramifications of the proposals. When anyone produced a concrete proposal, House snatched it to extract himself from the chaos. If House had been present in earlier discussions, he might have possessed a better understanding of the reparations problem.

House agreed to the omission of any time limit on the payment of reparations. He did not understand what he had accepted. After Wilson returned to the council, he did not reverse this decision, but plunged into the quarrels over the Rhineland and the Saar. Here he was willing to battle for his cause without considering the cost.

The French demanded the German frontier at the Rhine River with an Allied occupation of the left bank. The French were seeking to lay the basis for the creation of a separate state in the Rhineland. Again the experts failed to find agreement. In the Council of Four, Lloyd George opposed the Rhine frontier fearing the effect on the balance of power. From Wilson, he obtained a pledge to join in an Anglo-American guarantee of French security.

Clemenceau accepted the guarantee but demanded a thirty-

[8] Seth P. Tillman, *Anglo-American Relations at the Paris Peace Conference, 1919*, 244.

year Allied occupation of the Rhineland and complete German demilitarization in the area fifty kilometers east of the Rhine. Wilson and Lloyd George still were opposed.

Battle over the Rhineland was joined in earnest on March 27 when Wilson asked for moderation. They must not destroy Germany. "Our greatest error would be to give her some powerful reasons to wish one day to take her revenge." He did not fear "wars prepared by secret plots of governments but conflicts created by the discontent of populations." Clemenceau was more fearful that the League of Nations would lack the means to give France security against Germany.[9]

In the afternoon Wilson proposed to accept demilitarization coupled with the Anglo-American guarantee. But Clemenceau viewed this as a temporary measure and asked to include it within the Covenant of the League of Nations. Wilson refused, claiming that Britain and the United States would take whatever action the league recommended in case of aggression against a member of the League of Nations.[10]

The question of the Rhineland became entwined with the French demand for annexation of the Saar, a small but significant industrial area. Wilson fought against annexation, arguing that the French claim lacked sufficient historical basis. Annexation would harm the principles upon which they were trying to base the peace settlement. Although he considered the French economic claims just, Wilson rejected any political claim.

Lloyd George warned that annexation might create another Alsace-Lorraine. He supported autonomy. If they tried to give the Germans justice, Clemenceau declared, "they will never pardon us; they will only seek an opportunity for revenge." He harangued the trio about the war and its effects on France. The Americans did not understand the French views, he complained, because they remained out of the war for three years.

On April 7, Wilson alarmed the peace conference when

[9] Mantoux, *Les délibérations*, I, 41–45.
[10] *Ibid.*, I, 50–51.

he ordered the liner *George Washington* prepared for a voyage to take him back to the United States. Negotiations over the Saar and the Rhineland were not progressing. Lloyd George seemed to be leaning towards the French view of the Saar question. When Wilson brought in a proposal for the Saar on April 9, he found his associates very receptive. The Saar would be administered for fifteen years by a League of Nations commission. At the end of this period, a plebiscite would determine its sovereignity.[11] Wilson's suggestion became the basis for the final treaty. He had won the battle to keep France from annexing the Saar.

A compromise soon followed on the Rhineland when Clemenceau agreed to a fifteen-year occupation of the territory coupled with demilitarization and an Anglo-American guarantee against German aggression.

In the arguments over the Polish problem, Wilson and Clemenceau allied against Lloyd George. Originally the commission delegated by the peace conference to study Poland had recommended the corridor separating East Prussia from Germany. Danzig would come under Polish rule. Lloyd George took up the fight against the inclusion of more than two million Germans in Poland. He also opposed including Danzig in Poland. "The Poles will govern badly . . . . There will be trouble; if the Germans in Poland revolt, there will be fighting. If Germany wants to intervene, will you dispatch troops to keep the Germans under the yoke of Poland?" Danzig ought to be a free port, and the Poles should remain "in Poland and the Germans in Germany."[12]

Wilson had great sentimental regard for the Poles. He admitted that the inclusion of so many Germans inside the Polish Corridor was unfortunate, but there was no alternative. Clemenceau thought only of the strategic and military advantages for France. Lloyd George distrusted the Poles; they had fought against the Allied armies until the end of the war.

[11] *Ibid.*, I, 70.
[12] *Ibid.*, I, 46–47.

At last Lloyd George brought Wilson to accept Danzig as a free city under a League of Nations high commissioner. Clemenceau did not long resist them. Lloyd George warned them not to insert anything in the peace treaty about Poland for which they would not fight. "France will make war tomorrow for Alsace if it is contested. But will we make war for Danzig?"[13] No one answered his question then. His answer came in 1939.

No question caused so much futile argument during the deliberations of the Council of Four than the Italian demand for Fiume and Dalmatia. Orlando had said little during the earlier meetings. On April 13, he insisted that nothing further should be done about Germany until the Italian claims were settled. Although these were unrelated to the German treaty, Wilson did not object because he imagined that the matter could be handled easily. Clemenceau was cool; Lloyd George was hostile.

Orlando admitted that he needed a favorable decision or his government might fall. He wanted the natural frontiers of the Alps up to the watershed line, "the natural frontier which God has given us." He did not care if foreigners were included, and he reminded his hearers of the Germans who would live in Poland and Czechoslovakia. He based his claims to Dalmatia and Fiume on the Roman Empire, the Treaty of Campo-Formio which Napoleon forced on Austria in 1797, and the Republic of Venice.

Earlier in the Peace Conference, Wilson had conceded to Italy the Brenner Pass in the Alps as the frontier for Italy with Austria although 250,000 Germans would come under Italian rule. Orlando was surprised at his refusal to yield any further on the Italian claims. The President saw no reason why Fiume should be attached to Italy. It would be contrary to the new principles which he was trying to introduce into international affairs. Italy did not need Dalmatia for defense because of the League of Nations. He had crossed the ocean to take Europe

13 *Ibid.*, I, 109–13, 197–202, 271–73.

from the old order which had caused this catastrophe. Here was the old way.

Clemenceau and Lloyd George were embarrassed because their governments had signed the Treaty of London in 1915 promising Italy sections of the Austro-Hungarian Empire. According to the treaty terms, Italy would obtain Dalmatia, Trieste, Tyrol, but not Fiume. This was the price paid to insure Italy's entrance into the war on the side of the Entente powers. In 1915 the Italian government imagined that some of the Austro-Hungarian Empire would survive the war. Italy wanted to be able to dominate the Adriatic Sea, and these areas plus adjoining islands might accomplish the task.

When Orlando insisted on the Treaty of London plus Fiume, Wilson objected. American intervention had nothing to do with the Treaty of London, the President declared. Without American help there would not have been any victory. Wilson exclaimed: "When we entered the war, we declared the principles which directed our action and these principles have been acclaimed, not only by the small, oppressed nations, but by people of the great nations, who recognize their profound aspirations." When he wrote the Fourteen Points, said Wilson, he was not writing his own conscience but the views of the people of the United States. These principles were identical with the feelings of all the Allied nations. If they did not apply these principles, they would produce hatreds which would cause future troubles. The President proclaimed that the United States would not be associated with the Treaty of London. Lloyd George dolefully observed that they had reached the "most difficult situation that had faced [the council] since the beginning of the conference." Orlando broke into tears.[14] A summit conference had reached an impasse.

Clemenceau and Lloyd George feared that Wilson might not sign the German treaty because of his quarrel with Orlando. Then the conference would collapse. They pleaded with Or-

[14] *FRUS*, V, 80–101; Mantoux, *Les délibérations*, I, 237–45, 277–98.

lando to avoid antagonizing Wilson because European economy needed American financial aid. The President had gone much further in understanding European views than they had believed possible. Clemenceau reminded the Italian premier how he had compromised on his demands for Germany to satisfy Wilson; Orlando could do the same. If Wilson's policies prevailed, Orlando retorted, there would be revolution in Italy.

Wilson helped the quarrel by issuing a declaration to the Italian people over Orlando's head. He claimed that he had to prevent Italy giving her story to the world first. He must clarify the situation, dissipate misunderstandings, and indicate the views of the United States. On April 23, Wilson issued his manifesto calling for the Italian people to subscribe to the new order as outlined in his Fourteen Points. If Italy adhered to these principles, however, Fiume could not belong to Italy.[15]

Wilson's tactics provoked a storm in Italy and forced Orlando to hasten to Rome for some political fence-mending. His colleagues were delighted to see him depart. Lloyd George and Clemenceau considered alienating Wilson more serious than alienating Orlando. The trio did nothing to encourage the Italian premier to return. Without Orlando in Paris delaying the peace conference, they pushed on with the German treaty.

When Orlando returned on May 7, the battle began again. At last Wilson accepted Fiume as a free city; after five years a plebiscite would determine its sovereignty. The President steadfastly refused to recognize the Treaty of London. Orlando's government fell on June 21 chiefly because he could not obtain Fiume.

On June 28, 1919, after the Germans had signed the Versailles Treaty, the last matter discussed by Wilson, Clemenceau, and Lloyd George before they parted forever was a final note to Italy over her claims.[16]

[15] *FRUS,* V, 216–17; Mantoux, *Les délibérations,* I, 300–306, 314, 329, 355–67.

[16] FRUS, V, 426–36, 452–59; *ibid.,* VI, 738–39, 759–62; Mantoux, *Les délibérations* I, 468–74, 476–82; *ibid.,* II, 553–55.

Taking advantage of the confusion within the Council of Four over the Italian claims, the Japanese demanded that the German concessions in China be transferred to them. These had been obtained by Germany in 1899 from the Chinese government in the Shantung Peninsula. Again wartime treaties returned to haunt Clemenceau and Lloyd George. When Japanese naval help was needed during the war, Britain and France promised to support Japan's claims at the peace conference. Now they remained loyal to their promise.

Wilson complained that the Japanese sought to acquire more rights in China than Germany originally possessed. The American public would be sorely distressed at such tactics. Despite his complaints, Wilson never opposed the Japanese demands as he had the Italian. He alleged that there was a profound difference: Italy had no right to make such claims because Austria-Hungary no longer existed and had been replaced by independent nations. Actually he feared that vigorous opposition to the Japanese demands might drive Japan to reject membership in the League of Nations and create an "abyss between the Orient and the Occident."[17] Japanese troops had already occupied the Shantung area; they could not be ejected except by force, which no one volunteered to do. Neither Clemenceau nor Lloyd George would support him.

Wilson extracted a promise from the Japanese to hand back the Shantung Peninsula to the Chinese, retaining only the German economic privileges. He hoped to obtain justice for the Chinese through the League of Nations. But the Chinese were so dissatisfied that they refused to sign the Versailles Treaty.

The Japanese claims had little direct bearing on the German treaty. The Italian claims had none whatsoever. Neither would they have been discussed except for the loose organization of the Council of Four. Other questions with little direct bearing on the Versailles Treaty hampered the work of the council: How to stop the Poles from fighting the Ukraines? What

[17] *Ibid.*, I, 336.

would be the spheres of influence for Britain and France in Syria? Should the Polish government be required to teach Yiddish in government schools? Should they send boots to Russia? How to stop the Czechs and Hungarians from fighting? What to do about those Russians?

The Russian problem perplexed the council. Reliable information was lacking. Could the White Russian forces be trusted? Because they were fighting the Bolsheviks, various White Russian armies asked the Allied powers to furnish them with money and supplies. Frustrated by these demands, Wilson exclaimed that Russia should be left to the Bolsheviks. "They can stew in their own juice," he cried, "until circumstances make them wiser." The council feared that unemployed German soldiers would take service under the Bolsheviks and introduce them to German efficiency and techniques. After lengthy discussions, the council offered to give munitions, supplies, and food to Admiral A. V. Kolchak, one of the White Russian leaders. He had to accept certain conditions including free elections and land reform. When Kolchak agreed, the council promised aid. But it was too late. Before the end of June, Kolchak's army had collapsed.[18]

An Indian delegation interrupted the council's work on May 17. Their cause was unrelated to the treaty. In full array came the Maharajah of Binanie, the Right Honorable Lord Sinha, His Highness the Aga Khan, Aftab Ahmad, Yusuf Ali, and the Right Honorable E. S. Montagu, British secretary of state for India. Speaking for the Indian Moslems, these gentlemen objected to the plans to dismember the Ottoman Empire and eject the sultan from Constantinople. The Aga Khan reminded Wilson of point twelve in his Fourteen Points, calling for "secure sovereignty" for Turkey. The Council was much impressed by the delegation. Later Wilson admitted that he had forgotten

[18] *FRUS*, V, 529, 909–11; *ibid.*, VI, 73–75, 212–13, 321–23; Mantoux, *Les délibérations*, I, 20, 80; *ibid.*, II, 324–25.

mentioning Turkey in his Fourteen Points. The council turned to more important matters.

No action of the Council of Four became so notorious and created such controversy as Article 231 of the Versailles Treaty.

> The Allied and Associated Governments affirm and Germany accepts the responsibility of Germany and her allies for causing all the loss and damage to which the Allied and Associated governments and their nationals have been subjected as a consequence of the war imposed upon them by the aggression of Germany and her allies.

German critics alleged that the Council of Four had placed sole responsibility for causing the war on Germany. The council drafted the article for a different purpose, but in 1919, few in Paris doubted German guilt in causing the war.

After 1919, those who advocated revising the Treaty of Versailles singled out Article 231 as the "war guilt clause." Denounced by revisionist historians it became the subject of countless speeches and articles by German politicians and journalists.

Article 231 originated in a compromise between Wilson's wish to exclude war costs and the desire of Clemenceau and Lloyd George to appease their tax payers who wanted the defeated to pay for the war. The trio agreed that the Germans should recognize their theoretical obligation to pay war costs as well as damages. "But without a doubt," Clemenceau observed, "Germany cannot pay all that she ought to pay." The final wording of the article confirmed the view of the American expert, Norman Davis: "Germany is morally responsible for the war and all of its consequences, and she is juridically responsible for the damage to goods and to persons."[19]

The council adopted the article on April 5 with little discussion. House was substituting for the ailing Wilson who certainly approved. No one then imagined the repercussions of

[19] *Ibid.,* I, 151–52; Tillman, *Anglo-American Relations,* 246–48.

25

Article 231. In time it became the focus for German hatred of the Versailles Treaty.

After the draft treaty had been released to the world and public opinion became known, only Lloyd George attempted to alter the terms. Early in May, British and American experts freely criticized the draft treaty. Their objections had more impact on Lloyd George than on Wilson. The President held the first and last meeting of the entire American delegation to discuss the treaty. Unless the treaty could be proven unjust towards Germany, Wilson had no desire to change it. He believed that the British should have been more concerned earlier with the contents of the draft treaty.

The British delegation, reinforced by telegrams from members of Parliament, influenced Lloyd George to propose changes in the terms of the treaty. Lloyd George obtained a plebiscite in Upper Silesia, part of the Polish Corridor which had a large German population. Wilson assented reluctantly. Although Lloyd George requested changes in the reparations clauses, he rejected Wilson's proposal to set a fixed sum of reparations at $25,000,000,000. Wilson failed to battle as fiercely for this change as he had done earlier to stop Orlando's bid for Fiume. He accepted the suggestion of Lloyd George to allow the Germans four months in which to submit a lump sum, but they would have to accept the treaty without a fixed sum for reparations.

Lloyd George also won agreement favoring early admission of Germany to the League of Nations. At his instigation, changes were made in the terms of the Rhineland occupation. If Germany displayed good will and insured fulfillment of her obligations, the occupation would be terminated within less than fifteen years.

More changes could have been made by Wilson and Lloyd George if they had been willing to try harder, but differences in personality and character prevented concerted action. Because he believed that the Welshman was motivated by expediency and not by principle, the President declined further alterations in a treaty which he considered just.[20]

Regardless of the question under discussion—Poland, reparations, German disarmament—the council was haunted by the fear that the German delegation would not sign the treaty. Without a signed peace treaty, the world would be in chaos, they thought. When the French government intercepted telegrams dispatched to Berlin by the German delegation, the members of the council eagerly read them for any indication that the Germans would sign.[21]

Wilson forced the council to accept full occupation if the Germans refused to sign. Marshal Foch, Allied commander-in-chief, was asked for his occupation plans. The council wanted the armies to move against Berlin, overthrow the government, and create a German government that would sign the peace treaty. Foch balked because he had only thirty-nine divisions; daily, American and British troops left Europe. Because he feared the German population, he would be obliged to detach enough troops to control sixty-five million people. Instead of marching directly on Berlin, Foch wanted to separate the southern German states by obtaining their signatures to the treaty. The council was aghast. In May, Foch had said he needed only a week to begin the march on Berlin. Now he evaded every question about his change of mind.

On June 20, Foch brought the other Allied commanders before the council: General Ugo Cavallero, Marshal Philippe Petain, General Maxime Weygand, General Tasker H. Bliss, General Sir Henry Wilson, and General William Robertson. All were united behind Foch. Without reinforcements the Allied armies could not reach Berlin; the southern states must be detached. Allied armies could only reach the Weser River; thereafter they must be reinforced or the treaty must be changed.

[20] *Ibid.*, 356–62.
[21] Mantoux, *Les délibérations,* II, 53, 72, 110.

Beyond the Weser a new war could be fought by 750,000 German troops. Without reinforcements the Allied armies could not reach their goal. The generals impressed the council. Before the council could find a solution, the German government accepted the treaty.[22]

The council hesitated to use force even when the Germans broke the armistice. In violation of the armistice terms, on June 21, German crews scuttled naval vessels interned at Scapa Flow. News of the scuttling left the council bewildered. Lawyers, who were consulted, held that because this action violated the armistice, reparations could be required and punishment meted out by Allied armies and navies.

Reports that other Germans had burned captured French flags enraged Clemenceau. France had been insulted. Both violations of the armistice had been ordered by the German government. The Premier reminded his colleagues of reports that German generals were preparing to resist the cession of territory in Upper Silesia to Poland. "Even before the Germans sign the Treaty, they are preparing to violate it!" Clemenceau exclaimed. These acts proved to him how difficult it would be to make the Germans execute the treaty once it was signed. He demanded military action to show the Allied intention to force respect of the treaty. Clemenceau proposed to seize Essen after the treaty had been signed because there factories still produced cannon.

Wilson and Lloyd George were sympathetic but cautious. The President rejected the use of force because then the war would be renewed. All their toil over the peace treaty would be in vain. Lloyd George dreaded an unfavorable British reaction if the Allies seized a German town after the peace treaty had been signed. He begged Clemenceau to be satisfied with some compensation more fitting to the violations.

[22] *FRUS,* V, 537–40; *ibid.,* VI, 501–509, 521, 543–52; Mantoux *Les délibérations,* II, 22–24, 430–38, 442–44, 458–67.

Clemenceau insisted that Germany could not resist. If they permitted these violations, others would follow. "The moment will come," he warned, "when we will be separated, when we will have no more soldiers, and then Germany will do whatever she wishes." Yet he assured his colleagues that France would do nothing alone. Clemenceau lost the argument. The council declared a breach of the armistice; they would exact reparations only after an investigation. By then, they prayed, the treaty would be signed.[23]

If Germany had not signed, the council would have been in a perplexing position. Lloyd George was under heavy pressure from his coalition government to conclude a quick peace; Wilson was eager to return home; Clemenceau would have risked an occupation, but the generals would not. Perhaps, passive resistance by Germany, coupled with a refusal to sign, would have won more from the Allies than signing the treaty with loud objections.

The summit conference of 1919 was hampered by the strengths as well as weaknesses of the four leaders. Their personality differences made negotiation sometimes impossible, and once an impasse had been reached, there was no authority to which they could refer for a new viewpoint or a compromise. To bring together four men of dissimilar backgrounds, conflicting personalities, and opposing viewpoints and expect them to rebuild the world through intimate negotiations was to force on them a task worthy of saints.

They showed their inexperience by failing to plan for a summit conference before the peace conference assembled, and they allowed events to force them into this new method. Once committed to that type of conference, they should have divested themselves of the duties of Supreme War Council. They could not write a peace treaty and at the same time tidy up the world.

[23] *FRUS*, VI, 588, 606, 613–14, 617–20, 641–44, 648–53, 656–63, 678, 695–96; Mantoux, *Les délibérations*, II, 482–85, 494–501, 503–10, 521.

Either would have been enough and would have required discipline, strictly defined goals, and a rigid agenda.

Without prior planning, too much work was thrown directly at the Council of Four in the first weeks of its work. Many problems should have been screened before coming to the council's attention. Through experience they learned to refer new subjects either to the foreign ministers or to a committee of experts.

The exclusion of the smaller nations from the summit conference was justified because these nations were interested in their own particular loot. Often their greed was proportionately greater than that of the major powers.

Never was there any intention to permit changes by the full conference because the council had labored too long for the conference to alter their work. Revisions would only prolong the peace conference, and the council was compelled to produce a signed peace treaty. Additional alterations might bring a German rejection of the treaty, and to live without a peace treaty was unthinkable.

The council spent too much time on minute details. The Premier of the Republic of France, the President of the United States of America, the Prime Minister of Great Britain, and the Premier of the Kingdom of Italy all had more important tasks than to debate whether "military" should be inserted before "law"; or whether to delete "you will not be surprised to learn" and substitute "in reply we beg to say."

Throughout the story of the Council of Four, there was an expectation that the United States would honor a treaty drawn up and signed by Wilson. He was responsible for more in the treaty than merely the Covenant of the League of Nations. Too often have American historians ignored this fact and condemned the Versailles Treaty as a piece of Anglo-French knavery, neglecting Wilson's role.

Clemenceau and Lloyd George, fearing that the United States government would not ratify the treaty, made concessions to Wilson. But the United States Senate would not support the

President's work in the summit conference of 1919. Such were the perils of the summit conference. Nevertheless, this summit conference set a precedent because in the succeeding decades, the practice of personal diplomacy by chiefs of state at the summit increased.

3

The Czechoslovak Crisis

For the next twenty years there were high-level conferences but none had the prestige of the leaders in the Council of Four until the Munich Conference of 1938. Then the heads of the French, British, German, and Italian governments assembled in Munich because of an international crisis involving Czechoslovakia and Nazi Germany.

The Paris Peace Conference had not solved the German problem. The Versailles Treaty was resented, particularly Article 231. A new republican government went through the motions of enforcing the Versailles Treaty. In 1923, French and Belgian troops occupied the Ruhr in an unsuccessful attempt to enforce the treaty.

Germany endured inflation and then enjoyed prosperity

until the collapse of the economy in 1931. Capitalizing on the German torment, Austrian-born Adolf Hitler made the National Socialists the largest political party in Germany. On January 30, 1933, Hitler became chancellor of Germany. He had never concealed his aims: destruction of the Versailles Treaty, German rearmament, authoritarian government, persecution of the Jews, and the extension of the German frontiers.

In his youth, Hitler had been infected with Pan-Germanism: the union of all Germans in a great empire regardless of political boundaries. Great was his hatred of Czechoslovakia whose frontiers encompassed Germans living in the Sudetenland, western Czechoslovakia.

The Sudetenland had been a favored area of the Austro-Hungarian Empire. Ancestors of the Sudeten Germans had begun to migrate from Germany in the twelfth century. Empress Maria Theresa and her son Joseph invited more German immigrants to settle in western areas of Bohemia in the eighteenth century. During World War I, the Sudetenland provided many loyal soldiers for the armies of Franz Josef. Before the war ended, the Sudetenland had become a part of the new Czechoslovakia.

Although the Paris Peace Conference studied the Sudeten minority problem, for reasons of national economy the old frontier was retained with slight changes. Yet many politicians in Western Europe came to believe that the Versailles Treaty had torn the Sudetenland from Imperial Germany.

In the new nation, the Sudetens lost their position of dominance in Bohemia which they had enjoyed under the Hapsburg Monarchy. A small Nazi party in the Sudetenland had little importance until after Hitler came to power and began to send subsidies. Then Nazi propagandists spread tales of Sudeten mistreatment at the hands of the Czechs. But in Europe the Sudetens were one of the best treated minorities.

Until he had destroyed the armament restrictions placed on Germany by the Versailles Treaty, Hitler refrained from aggressive action.[1] In 1935, Hitler announced German rearmament in violation of the Versailles Treaty. The victors of 1918 only protested. Hitler challenged them again in 1936 when he ordered German troops into the Rhineland which had been demilitarized in accordance with the Versailles Treaty. No nation would enforce the treaty.

In a secret conference on November 5, 1937, Hitler informed his ministers that Germany must expand into Czechoslovakia and Austria because of the need for space. Although he expected feeble opposition from France and Britain, force might be required.[2] By December 7, plans were under way for an attack on Czechoslovakia if circumstances were favorable.[3] Before these plans could be used, Hitler seized an opportunity to achieve *Anschluss* (union) with Austria on March 11, 1938. Now German territory surrounded western Czechoslovakia on three sides. Czechoslovak fortifications in the Sudetenland could be enveloped from the former Austrian frontier.

On March 28, 1938, Hitler ordered Konrad Henlein, leader of the Sudeten Nazi Party, to raise unacceptable demands with the Czechoslovak government over the question of Sudeten minority rights. Hitler never intended that the demands should be met. By refusing to accede to Hitler's ever changing demands, the Czechoslovak government would appear stubborn to those in Britain and France who had little desire to defend Czechoslovakia.[4]

Henlein's demands on the Czechoslovak government aimed either at disintegration of the state or an autonomous Sudetenland which the Nazis could dominate. President Eduard Beneš of Czechoslovakia was unwilling to grant every concession lest

[1] Conference of Ministers, February 8, 1933, *Documents on German Foreign Policy* (hereafter cited at *DGFP*), Series C, I, 35–37.

[2] Hossbach Memorandum, November 10, 1937, *ibid.*, Series D, I, 29–39.

[3] Directive by the commander-in-chief of the *Wehrmacht*, December 21, 1937, *ibid.*, Series D, VII, 635–38.

[4] Report of Henlein's audience with Hitler, March 28, 1938, *ibid.*, Series D, II, 197–202.

other minorities request similar treatment. Only Hitler would profit from the resulting chaos.

No nation was sincerely willing to back Czechoslovakia against Hitler. Most of Europe embraced neutrality. Poland and Hungary coveted portions of Czechoslovakia. The Soviet government made impractical suggestions knowing they would be discarded. British and French memories of the 1914–18 blood bath were still too fresh.[5]

Neither Britain nor France was ready for a war over Czechoslovakia. The French high command planned only to man the Maginot Line, a series of concrete and steel fortifications constructed at great expense along the western frontiers of Germany. The commander of the antiquated French Air Force expected the German *Luftwaffe* to wrest control of the air within two weeks after the outbreak of war.

The British army was strong enough for a colonial war but not a European conflict. The chain of radar stations was incomplete. The Royal Air Force was short of modern aircraft and trained personnel. On March 28, 1938, the British chiefs of staff informed Prime Minister Neville Chamberlain that Britain needed time to rearm for war because her armed forces were unprepared.

Chamberlain did not think that Czechoslovakia could be saved from German invasion. He would not involve his country in a war over Czechoslovakia unless there were prospects for a quick victory. Of these he saw none. Because Czechoslovakia could not be saved, he would not give any guarantee.[6] He was also a firm believer in the justice of the Sudeten cause.

The French government, headed by Edouard Daladier, was joined to Czechoslovakia by an alliance. Fearful of facing Germany alone, unhappy with the Czech alliance, Daladier handed over to Chamberlain the fate of France.

[5] Keith Eubank, *Munich*, 10, 31–32.
[6] Chamberlain to his sister, March 20, 1938, quoted in Ian Macleod, *Neville Chamberlain*, 224.

During the spring and summer of 1938, Chamberlain and Daladier labored to force the Beneš government to concede to the Sudeten wishes. Whatever Beneš and Czechoslovak Prime Minister Milan Hodža offered, however, the Sudeten leaders somehow found unacceptable.

Rumors of German troop movements along the German frontier led the Czech cabinet to order a partial mobilization on May 20. Although the French cabinet pledged support of Czechoslovakia, and the British promised to aid France, neither was happy. Both were relieved when German declarations of innocence proved true.

On May 28, Hitler informed his associates that it was his "unshakable will that Czechoslovakia shall be wiped off the map."[7] On May 30, he signed a directive ordering increased preparations for an attack on Czechoslovakia by October 1.

By midsummer many observers reported German preparations for war. Frightened at the mounting danger to peace, Chamberlain dispatched Walter Runciman to Prague ostensibly to act as a mediator between Prague and the Sudetens. A wealthy shipowner, he had no experience in diplomacy. Actually he was charged with the task of compelling the Czechoslovak government to grant the wishes of the Sudeten Nazis. Despite Runciman's efforts, the Sudeten Nazis always found objections to whatever concessions were proposed.

Sudeten Nazis used Hitler's speech at the Nürnberg party rally on September 12 as an excuse to riot and loot. Acting swiftly, the Czechoslovak government restored order, but the Sudeten leaders broke off negotiations with Prague. Henlein fled across the German frontier and from there issued a call for the Sudetens to be taken home to the *Reich*.

Paris implored London to find a way out of the crisis lest France have to fulfill her obligations to Czechoslovakia. From Berlin, Ambassador Neville Henderson begged London for action before Hitler marched. Chamberlain resolved to fly to

[7] Schmundt file, *Nazi Conspiracy and Aggression*, IV, 309–10, 314.

Germany and meet with Hitler. Through personal diplomacy, war could be avoided and millions saved from death.

At their meeting on September 15 at Berchtesgaden, Hitler threatened war unless the Sudetens were returned to the *Reich*. Using self-determination, the Sudetenland should be ceded to Germany. Such a solution seemed suitable to Chamberlain who then returned to London. There, on September 18, he consulted with Daladier and Georges Bonnet, the French foreign minister. Chamberlain brought them to accept his view that the Sudetenland should be ceded to Germany in an orderly manner with enough time provided for the peaceful transfer of property and population.[8]

Both governments requested Prague to accept their proposal that the Sudeten areas with more than 50 per cent German population should be ceded to Germany with an international commission handling the transfer of people and their possessions. Britain would join in an international guarantee of the remainder of Czechoslovakia.

When the Czechoslovak government rejected the proposal, it was transformed into an ultimatum. Unless the plan was accepted unconditionally, Chamberlain would cease his efforts, and, if war came, the armies of France would not march. On September 21 the Czechoslovak government capitulated to the Anglo-French ultimatum.

When Chamberlain conferred with Hitler at Godesberg on September 22, the German leader had fresh demands. Polish and Hungarian claims to Czechoslovak territory must be satisfied. The Sudetenland must be ceded immediately and occupied by the German army. Then Hitler would hold a plebiscite. The occupation must begin by September 26 and be completed by September 28. Every installation, military and civilian, must remain intact. Neither cattle, food, nor raw materials could be

[8] Chamberlain's notes of his talk with Hitler, September 15, 1938, *Documents on British Foreign Policy* (hereafter cited as *DBFP*), Third Series, II, 338–41; memorandum of a conversation between Hitler and Chamberlain, September 15, 1938, *DGFP*, Series D, II, 786–98.

removed. Chamberlain complained that the cession and occupation would arouse Czech resistance and lead to war. To pacify the Prime Minister, Hitler changed the date of occupation to October 1.[9]

Czechoslovakia rejected these conditions and commenced mobilization. With heavy hearts, the French cabinet promised support. The Chamberlain government resolved to stand by France. The Prime Minister so informed Hitler by messenger.

Hitler displayed little interest in the message. He declared that Britain and France would have to attack Germany, because in the west Germany would wage a defensive war only. But the Anglo-French military staffs had no plans for an aggressive war against Germany, thus leaving German troops free to take the offensive against Czechoslovakia in the east.

Chamberlain continued his search for a formula to appease Hitler and avoid the slaughter of millions. On September 27 the Prime Minister proposed a Czech evacuation of the Sudetenland according to a time table that would place German troops in the area no later than October 31. The same day, Hitler dispatched a conciliatory letter to Chamberlain promising to guarantee the remnant of Czechoslovakia.

Heartened by the apparent change in Hitler's attitude, Chamberlain telegraphed the *Führer* that he was anxious to return to Germany and examine the Sudeten problem with Czech, French, and Italian representatives. Independent of Chamberlain, Georges Bonnet drafted a plan which offered Hitler greater concessions. Both Chamberlain and Bonnet assured Hitler that he could obtain whatever he desired from Czechoslovakia because their governments would be the guarantors.

Benito Mussolini, the Italian dictator, feared war almost as much as Chamberlain and Daladier. He implored Hitler to post-

[9] Minutes of conversations between Chamberlain and Hitler at Godesberg, September 22–24, 1938, *ibid.*, 870–79, 898–908; *DBFP*, Third Series, II, 463–73, 499–508.

pone the attack on Czechoslovakia and accept Chamberlain's proposal for a four-power conference.

In the afternoon of September 28, Hitler invited Daladier, Chamberlain, and Mussolini to come to Munich the next day for a conference over Czechoslovakia. Hitler issued the invitation because he had nothing to lose, and, if he failed to obtain his desires, his army was ready to invade Czechoslovakia. The conference would be a great victory for him.

Although France had an alliance with Czechoslovakia, neither Beneš nor a representative was invited to the conference. Because he certainly would have raised objections and prolonged the discussions, no one wanted him there.

The Soviet Union was pledged to aid Czechoslovakia if France acted first, and there was also an alliance between France and the Soviet Union. Nevertheless, neither the French nor the British wanted Joseph Stalin at the Munich Conference. Because no one wanted him there, he did not receive an invitation, and he was probably delighted to be ignored.

Of the quartet who met in the *Führerhaus* in Munich on September 29, 1938, only the Italian dictator, Benito Mussolini, had any diplomatic experience. Stuffed with his own conceit but frightened at Italy's lack of preparation, he wanted only to avoid war. The fate of Czechoslovakia did not interest him.

Daladier, a former history professor and an honest soldier, yearned to be rid of French obligations to defend Czechoslovakia. He feared for his political future, which he had rebuilt with care after its collapse in 1934. He at least could grasp the danger to the balance of power.

Chamberlain desired to remove roadblocks to peace, a process he called "appeasement"—then a respectable word. He never meant surrender but only service to those who were annoyed by the nasty Versailles Treaty and who might precipitate a world war. He had a long and honorable political career without experience in diplomacy; his training in business colored his views on diplomacy and foreign policy. Face-to-face meetings in private between statesmen should solve problems and bring peace. Chamberlain was almost Marxist in his belief that once confidence of the business world was restored by the possibility of peace, the economic rewards would so gratify Hitler that he would be happy. In his travels to and from Germany, Chamberlain searched for a formula that would appease Hitler and avoid the slaughter of millions.

Hitler had no experience in negotiating with equals but preferred to threaten, scream, and frighten his opponents into surrender. His antics alarmed statesmen who feared that resistance to his demands might push him into war from whence there would be no return. They also feared the onrush of Communism in the backwash of war.

Hitler intended that this conference would be to his glory, but if there were resistance, he would march. The conference must not become a mere legal ceremony, glorifying peaceful diplomatic procedures. Instead, it must exalt his power and might.

Hitler joined Mussolini for a conference on September 29 as soon as the *Duce's* train crossed the frontier. During the trip to Munich, Hitler raved about the British and French, swearing never to cede to the democracies but to strike when they were disorganized. He seemed to expect that the conference would fail and that war would break out, bringing the destruction of Czechoslovakia.

Unlike Hitler and Mussolini, Chamberlain and Daladier journeyed to the conference separately. Never did they confer privately on joint strategy to be used in the conference. Their failure to consult only made Hitler's task easier.

· 4 ·

Munich, 1938

THE MUNICH CONFERENCE opened at 12:45 in the afternoon in the *Führerhaus*. Hitler thanked the other heads of government for accepting his invitation. Then he launched into a tale of Czechoslovak iniquity which threatened the peace of Europe. As spokesman for the Sudetens, Hitler demanded that the Czechoslavak government fulfill the promise to cede territory to Germany. Any delay in solving the problem would be a crime because there seemed no end to the flood of Sudeten refugees. Despite the agreement that the Sudetenland should be ceded to Germany, Hitler wanted a plebiscite to determine how much land would ultimately be ceded. He must have action. No longer would he tolerate Prague's delay. The occupation would not be a problem because it would be accomplished within one week.

Chamberlain thanked Hitler for the invitation to a conference which would give Europe a chance to breathe. He was convinced that, with speed and the necessary spirit, good results would follow.

Mussolini also wanted speed. He presented a memorandum as a basis for discussion; the memorandum had been drafted in the German Foreign Office, and a copy had been handed to him by Hitler on the train.

Daladier thanked Hitler for the invitation and for the opportunity for a personal meeting. He found Mussolini's proposal admirable and accepted it as the basis for discussion, as did Chamberlain.

The German Foreign Office memorandum, which Mussolini presented, called for the evacuation and the cession of the Sudetenland to begin on October 1 and to be completed by October 10. France, Italy, and Britain would guarantee that no property would be destroyed. International committees would arrange for the evacuation and demarcation of the final frontier. Chamberlain and Daladier overlooked the obvious similarity to the Godesberg demands so eager were they for an agreement.

Chamberlain and Daladier asked for a Czech representative to be present in the next room for consultation and to insure that the Czechs would evacuate the Sudetenland by October 10. Daladier vowed that his government would never permit the Czechs to procrastinate.

Hitler scorned assurances from the Prague government. Only Czech acceptance of the proposal interested him. He was attracted to the guarantee that Czechoslovakia would comply. To obtain the Czechoslavak government's approval on every detail would prolong the conference. Hitler dismissed the request for a Czech representative with the announcement that no Czech was immediately available to speak with authority for the Prague government.

As a good businessman, Chamberlain raised questions about significant details. What power would the international commission possess? When the Sudeten territory had been evacuated, what authority would prevail? Were farmers to be expelled and forced to leave their cattle behind?

Hitler exploded. German laws would be applied in the evacuated territory. The Czechs must not drive away German cattle. More important, however, was this a purely German-Czech quarrel or a European problem? If it was of concern to Europe, should not the great powers use their authority and assume responsibility for the transfer. If the Czechs would not comply, then force alone could solve the problem.

Chamberlain accepted the time limit and the need for the powers to settle the problem. They must insure that obstinate Czechs would not repudiate the proposal. At his request, Mussolini's proposal was distributed among the conferees who adjourned about 3:00 P.M. to study it.

The recess offered a chance for Anglo-French planning. Chamberlain invited Daladier to confer in the Regina Hotel, where the British delegation was staying. Daladier rejected the invitation, and Chamberlain failed to go to Daladier's hotel and insist on a conference. Such distrust eased Hitler's task.

When the conference resumed about 4:30 P.M. Mussolini's memorandum was considered in greater detail. Chamberlain was reluctant to guarantee evacuation of the Sudetenland by October 10 as long as he was ignorant of the Czechoslovak attitude. Now Daladier refused to consult with the Czechs. He suggested consideration of geographical, economic, and political aspects of the Czech-Sudeten question. Hitler found Daladier's suggestion dangerous because Czechoslovakia owed its foundation to this idea. The structure was economically sound but weak in nationalism. According to Hitler, economic difficulties could be more easily overcome than those caused by nationalism.

The conference broke up into a babble of arguments over details. The harassed interpreter, Paul Schmidt, shouted to make himself heard. People wandered in and out of the conference room. Some had come to watch the confusion of a summit conference. The meeting assumed "the appearance of a waiting room at a railway station on the eve of a holiday weekend."[1]

Hitler rebuffed all attempts of the British delegation to insert detailed statements on compensating the Czech for property losses. For twenty years, he yelled, the Sudetens had paid for all this Czech property in taxes. The British were forced to accept a vague declaration that any question relating to the transfer should be referred to the international commission.

The proposals were turned over to a drafting committee, and the conference adjourned for dinner. A luxurious banquet had been prepared, but Chamberlain and Daladier declined the host's invitation. Again they failed to have any joint conference. The last session resumed about 10:00 P.M. for final study and correction of the work of the drafting committee. Early in the morning of September 30, the four statesmen signed the Munich Agreement.

The occupation would come in five stages and be completed by October 10. An international commission, with Czechoslovak representation, would decide on the final frontier and any areas requiring a plebiscite. Britain and France promised to guarantee the new frontiers against "unprovoked aggression." Germany and Italy agreed to guarantee the Czechoslovak frontiers after Polish and Hungarian minorities were satisfied. Another summit conference was promised within three months if the Polish and Hungarian minorities in Czechoslovakia were still dissatisfied.[2]

The Munich Conference had little planning. When the four heads of government were ready to sign the agreement, there was no ink. The conference lacked a chairman and an agenda; the principals wandered from one topic to another. In one area the conference was adequate: there was an abundance of food for those who wished to consume it.

[1] Ivone Kirkpatrick, *Mussolini, A Study in Power*, 384–85.
[2] Memoranda on the Munich Conference, September 29, 1938, *DGFP*, Series D, II, 1003–1008, 1011–14; Sir Horace Wilson's notes on the Munich Conference, September 29, 30, 1938, *DBFP*, Third Series, II, 627–29, 630–35.

Only Mussolini seemed to enjoy the conference, conferring here, chatting there, believing that his linguistic abilities were greater than they actually were. The peaceful outcome of the conference delighted him.

Hitler became unhappy when the conference achieved peace through negotiations instead of meek submission because of his threats. He did not use this type of diplomacy when he decided the fate of Czechoslovakia in 1939. Then the president of Czechoslovakia, Emil Hácha, after a tirade that almost caused him a heart attack, surrendered unconditionally.

Daladier was morose, sullen, and fearful of war. He did not stand up to Hitler during the conference because he knew that for France war was out of the question. When he departed for Munich, his chief of staff for air reminded him that, if war came, Paris would be destroyed in two weeks. Although he sensed the enormity of the defeat, the politician in him would not let him reveal the truth to the French when they gave him a hero's welcome. He chose to capitalize on public approval of the conference.

Chamberlain was motivated by an overwhelming desire to avoid war. To him, the Sudetenland was not worth the price of another world war with millions dead and wounded. In the Munich Conference, he tried to perform an onerous task that would lay the foundations for peace. He hoped to create a "Spirit of Munich" which would help keep the peace. The strategic defeat suffered by Britain at Munich was lost on him.

About 2:15 A.M., September 30, Chamberlain, at Daladier's insistence, met with the Czech minister in Berlin, Vojtéch Mastny, and Hubert Masařík, secretary to the Czech foreign minister. The unhappy Czech pair had been summoned to receive the terms of the Munich Agreement. Alexis St. Léger, secretary-general at the French Foreign Ministry, interpreted the agreement and answered questions while Daladier sat silent and Chamberlain yawned. The Czech diplomats learned that no answer would be expected because Czechoslovakia was considered to have accepted the agreement. A Czech representative was expected at the first meeting of the International Commission scheduled for 5:00 P.M., September 30.[3]

Mastny returned to Prague with the agreement that night. After an agonizing meeting, the Czech government surrendered and at 12.30 P.M., September 30, informed the Munich powers. To President Beneš no other alternative seemed possible. France, Britain, Germany, and Italy were leagued against Czechoslovakia, and the Soviet government would not fight for Czechoslovakia. By rejecting the Munich Agreement, the Czechoslovak government would be responsible for war and left without an ally. Perhaps a remnant of the nation might be saved by capitulation. At 12:30 P.M., Czechoslovakia accepted the agreement.

The signing of a private agreement with Hitler later in the morning of September 30 was Chamberlain's idea. He took no steps to inform the French about the impending conference. Through the promise to settle the future problems by consultations, such as the Munich Conference, Chamberlain hoped to have a series of summit conferences to keep the peace. Hitler was fooled into signing, for he did not realize that this old man took these words seriously.

At this summit conference, four men mortally wounded a nation that had been undefeated in war. Nothing comparable had been witnessed since the days of Frederick the Great, Catherine the Great, and Maria Theresa when they carved up Poland.

Many people who had denounced the Treaty of Versailles because Poland had received German lands now lauded the severance of the Sudetenland from Czechoslovakia as a great step on the road to European peace. In Germany, Chamberlain was almost as great a hero as Hitler. Daladier returned home to an hysterical, joyous reception. Frenchmen were delighted that peace had been saved at the expense of Czechoslovakia.

[3] Hubert Masařík's memorandum, September 29, 30, 1938, *Documents and Materials Relating to the Eve of the Second World War*, I, 264–67; Hubert Ripka, *Munich: Before and After*, 224–27.

Chamberlain and Daladier accepted the conference as a last means of avoiding another world war. Neither had the freedom to bargain with Hitler. Because both men had already conceded that the cause of the Sudetens was just, their only task was to satisfy Hitler. There was no attempt to consider the justice of the Sudeten cause on the basis of history and politics. German demands had been accepted, and the Czechs were compelled to surrender.

The goal of the Western leaders had been peace, but they lost that in 1939. Hitler gained dominance of Europe until his defeat in 1945, yet he lost the Munich Conference within a year. His occupation of the remainder of Czechoslovakia in March, 1939, shocked Britain and France, preventing additional concessions. If he had not moved so soon after the Munich Conference, Hitler probably could have had similar conferences with helpful concessions. After the fall of Prague, Chamberlain feared another Munich Conference unless he had prior assurance that Hitler would keep his word. In September, 1939, a proposed summit conference over the Polish question failed to materialize because of Hitler's actions in Czechoslovakia. In 1938, he had promised to have only Sudeten Germans in the *Reich*, yet in 1939 he forced Czechs into the *Reich*.[4]

The Munich Conference left Hitler disgusted with the Western leaders. He erred in believing that they would ultimately capitulate as they had done in September, 1938. If a summit conference met to consider Poland, Britain and France would again back down. But if war came, once Poland had been conquered they would cease fighting.

In September, 1938, a few in the West urged resistance to Hitler's demands even if war came. They were ignorant of Western weakness when Chamberlain and Daladier traveled to Munich. If Britain and France had fought in 1938, victory over Germany would have been doubtful. Thanks to the public and

[4] Keith Eubank, "The British Pledge to Poland: Prelude to War," *Southwestern Social Science Quarterly*, Vol. XLV, (March, 1965), 340–48.

47

the politicians, Britain and France lacked the planes, the means, and the will to invade Germany from the west.[5] Poland and Hungary were eager to carve up Czechoslovakia. No other nation, least of all the United States, would aid Czechoslovakia.

The evidence is slight to prove that Hitler was bluffing at the Munich Conference.[6] He was prepared for war against Czechoslovakia. No attack would come from the French, whose troops would sit in the Maginot Line. Britain lacked troops, artillery, tanks, and planes. Russia would not march. If the Munich Conference had failed, German troops could have ultimately overwhelmed Czechoslovakia.

Some German generals claimed that they were willing to oppose Hitler if the Anglo-French forces would fight first. Their past record did not make them worthy of trust. After the war, other German generals asserted at the Nürnberg trials that if war had come in 1938, Germany would have been defeated.[7] These assumptions were valid only if German troops could not invade Czechoslovakia and if Anglo-French forces swept into Germany from the west. The British and French staffs had neither the plans nor the means to invade Germany.[8]

The conference destroyed Chamberlain's policy of appeasement and made it seem nothing but surrender. Actually he had followed a policy which the Western nations had pursued since the French and Belgian troops had been pressed into evacuating the Ruhr in 1924.

The conference benefitted Soviet Russia whose leaders claimed that because they had been ignored, they were not responsible for the consequences. If the Czechs had resisted Hitler, they alleged, Russia would have supported them against the Nazis. But Russian help was always hedged with the conditions

[5] M. M. Postan, *British War Production*, 29–30, 70–72, 81–82; *Survey of International Affairs, 1938*, III, 545–55.

[6] A. J. P. Taylor, *Origins of the Second World War*, 166–67.

[7] William F. Shirer, *The Rise and Fall of the Third Reich*, 571–73; *Trials of the Major War Criminals*, X, 506–11; *ibid.*, XV, 361; *ibid.*, XX, 606.

[8] For a more detailed treatment of this aspect of the Munich Conference, consult Eubank, *Munich*, chap. 26.

that France must fight first. After 1945, the Munich Conference became ammunition for the Soviet propagandists who proclaimed that the capitalists, led by Chamberlain and Daladier, had betrayed Czechoslovakia at Munich in hopes of turning Hitler eastward toward the Soviet Union.

The Munich Conference and the agreement cannot be understood without knowledge of the preceding two decades of history when Europe labored to recover from the wounds of World War I. That statesmen would ever again plunge Europe into a general war seemed unthinkable. British voters applauded when their politicians deliberately weakened national defenses with deep cuts in the military budget. After the debacle of the Ruhr occupation in 1923, French governments were not disposed to enforce the Versailles Treaty alone. They assumed that the Poles, the Czechs, and the Russians would enforce the treaty while French troops sat secure and safe within the Maginot Line. Other nations looked to their own domestic affairs, leaving the peace-keeping to someone else.

If the Munich Agreement had been maintained by Hitler, the conference would have been acclaimed as an example of great statesmanship. Chamberlain and Daladier would have won niches in history as statesmen who avoided world war. Because Hitler went on to further aggression, Chamberlain and Daladier were denounced as appeasers, and whatever good they may have done was forgotten.

The Munich Conference crippled American diplomacy during the Cold War. The public and many politicians equated negotiation with appeasement which had come to mean "surrender." The practice of diplomacy has not fully recovered from this summit conference.

· 5 ·

In Search of a Conference

WORLD WAR II opened a new era in the history of the summit conference when leaders of the anti-German forces met to plan for the defeat of Hitler and later to lay the foundations for a new world order. Franklin D. Roosevelt, Winston Churchill, and Joseph Stalin, all amateur diplomats, met twice to deal with the problems of war and peace.

The careers of the trio had little in common. Stalin, a former seminary student, used the apparatus of the Communist Party to reach the pinnacle of political power in the Soviet Union. He liquidated all in the Communist Party, the Soviet government, and armed forces who might oppose his dictatorship. All Soviet life and government became subject to his will.

By signing the Nonaggression Pact of August 23, 1939,

Stalin helped Hitler begin World War II. In return for services rendered, Hitler bribed Stalin with eastern Poland, Estonia, Latvia, Finland, and Bessarabia as the Russian sphere of influence. Until Hitler's attack on the Soviet Union in June, 1941, Stalin remained loyal to the pact, shipping Hitler supplies and even providing Germany with a naval base near Murmansk.

Roosevelt was born into a wealthy upstate New York family. After graduating from Harvard University, he began his political career in the New York state legislature. From there he went to Washington as under-secretary of the Navy in Woodrow Wilson's administration. An attack of polio left him permanently crippled, but he overcame his grievous handicap and served two terms as governor of New York. His election to the Presidency in 1932 came at the height of the depression, when American foreign policy was isolationist. Roosevelt's foreign policy was pursued with isolationist congressmen always in mind.

Roosevelt rather disliked the British, and like many Americans unconsciously still fought the American Revolution. To Roosevelt and many of his fellow countrymen the British were admirable but cunning, always ready to swindle honest Americans out of their money. For king and empire they would stop at nothing.

Churchill was the son of a brilliant but often erratic politician and a beautiful American mother. After graduating from Sandhurst, he commenced a career which included cavalry service in India, newspaper work in the Boer War, the Sudan campaign of 1898, and the Spanish-American War. Churchill won his first parliamentary election in 1899. Although he held a variety of cabinet posts throughout his political career, he was often out of office for long periods. Brought back to the cabinet as first lord of the Admiralty in 1939, he became prime minister in 1940 when Chamberlain's government was brought down by the defeat in the Norwegian campaign.

Roosevelt and Churchill were eighth cousins once removed. During World War I, they met at dinner in Gray's Inn. Churchill forgot this meeting much to the annoyance of Cousin Franklin.[1] Both men met again in August, 1941, on shipboard in Argentia Bay off the Newfoundland coast. There they issued the Atlantic Charter, which was never intended to have the importance attributed to it. Soon after Japan attacked Pearl Harbor, Churchill came to the United States, where he addressed Congress and conferred with Roosevelt.

After the United States entered the war, Roosevelt expressed a desire to meet with Stalin but admitted that it was impractical because of the war. Before they could meet, relations among the Allies worsened. When Churchill visited Moscow in August, 1942, Stalin condemned Western failure to invade Europe that year as had been promised. Later he raised loud objections to United States diversion of supplies to the Pacific theater for use against the Japanese.

Somehow Roosevelt thought he had a way with Stalin. To Churchill he wrote:

> I know you will not mind my being brutally frank when I tell you that I think I can personally handle Stalin better than either your Foreign Office or my State Department. Stalin hates the guts of all your top people. He thinks he likes me better, and I hope he will continue to do so.[2]

Shortly after the Allied landings in North Africa in November, 1942, Roosevelt hinted to Stalin about the need for the three leaders to confer over the future Mediterranean campaign. Stalin ignored him and replied that staff consultations would suffice.

In December, 1942, Roosevelt came to the point. A conference of military leaders was insufficient because "they could come to no ultimate decision without our approval and secondly, because I think we should come to some tentative understanding about the procedures which should be adopted in the event

[1] John Gunther, *Roosevelt in Retrospect,* 14.
[2] Winston S. Churchill, *Hinge of Fate,* 201.

The Big Four attended the first summit conference, the Paris Peace Conference of 1919. From left to right are Vittorio Orlando, David Lloyd George, Georges Clemenceau, and President Woodrow Wilson. These heads of state drafted the Versailles Treaty with its controversial Article 231.

The pervading temper of the Munich Conference in 1938, "appeasement," conjured up ghosts which still linger to haunt Western diplomats. The participants of this gathering were, from left to right, Neville Chamberlain, Édouard Daladier, Adolf Hitler, Benito Mussolini, and Count Ciano.

Courtesy Wide World Photos

of a German collapse." For Roosevelt, the most compelling reason was his desire to talk with Stalin. He suggested a mid-January meeting in southern Algeria or Khartoum.[3]

Although Stalin welcomed the idea, he could not leave the Soviet Union, not even for a day. Roosevelt urged a meeting about March 1 in North Africa, but Stalin rejected this too. They would have to consult through correspondence.

In May, 1943, Roosevelt proposed a private meeting with Stalin that summer on either side of the Bering Straits; there would be as small a staff as possible. The President proposed to bring only Harry Hopkins, his special assistant, an interpreter, and a stenographer. Churchill would not be invited. Roosevelt advocated the meeting because he thought that if the German army cracked up during the winter campaign, there must be preparations for future Allied operations.[4]

Roosevelt wanted to omit Churchill from the conference lest his cousin endanger Allied unity. Shortly after World War I, Churchill had advocated severe treatment for the Soviet Union, and in August, 1942, he had a most unpleasant meeting with Stalin. Russian help was imperative for final victory. If Churchill acted too British, Stalin might retire in a huff and co-operate less with his allies, reasoned Roosevelt. A private meeting with Stalin without Churchill would give the President the opportunity to reassure him and win his confidence. Then Stalin would consent to a later conference with Churchill.

Stalin suggested a meeting during July or August in Fairbanks, Alaska. Refusing to be tied by any advance date, he would have the meeting called two weeks in advance. Because of the war, he would not be any more definite.[5]

Without knowing he was uninvited, Churchill wired Stalin in June that he would be happy to "go at any risk to any place

[3] Roosevelt to Stalin, December, 1942, *Foreign Relations of the United States, Diplomatic Papers, 1942*, III, 665–66.
[4] Roosevelt to Stalin, May 5, 1943, *Foreign Relations of the United States, The Conferences at Cairo and Teheran 1943* (hereafter cited as *Teheran*), 3–4.
[5] Stalin to Roosevelt, May 26, 1943, *ibid.*, 6–7.

that you and the President may agree upon." He suggested a meeting at Scapa Flow.[6]

Through Averell Harriman, American ambassador to the Soviet Union, Churchill learned that he was unwanted at a Stalin-Roosevelt meeting. He complained:

> The whole world is expecting and all our side are desiring a meeting of the three great powers at which, not only the political chiefs, but the military staffs would be present in order to plan the future war moves and, of course, search for the foundations of post war settlement. It would seem a pity to draw U. J. [Uncle Joe] 7,000 miles from Moscow for anything less than this.[7]

Roosevelt threw the blame on Stalin, alleging that the Soviet leader proposed that they meet alone for a "preliminary meeting." The President argued that there were advantages to such a private meeting: without military staffs they would be less prone to argue about the need for an Anglo-American invasion of France, and Stalin would be more frank about Japan, China, the Balkans, Finland, and Poland. Roosevelt wanted "to explore his thinking as fully as possible concerning Russia's post-war hopes and ambitions." As a sop to Churchill, he proposed a meeting afterwards in Quebec, followed by a conference between the three leaders later in the fall. He was certain that his view was the best.[8]

Churchill promised to raise no objections if Roosevelt could convince Stalin to come to a conference. In August, Stalin informed Roosevelt that he would not come to a meeting at any distance because he must go to the front and visit the troops. (Stalin strayed from the truth: he never visited troops at the front.) He wanted them to meet either in Astrakhan or Archangel. If Roosevelt could not come, a representative would be welcome. He wanted advance preparations, and he had no objection to Churchill's presence.

[6] Churchill to Roosevelt, June 13, 1943, *ibid.*, 8.
[7] Churchill to Roosevelt, June 25, 1943, *ibid.*, 10.
[8] Roosevelt to Churchill, June 28, 1943, *ibid.*, 11–12.

During their meeting in Quebec in August, 1943, Roosevelt and Churchill proposed to Stalin a meeting of the three leaders at Fairbanks. He rejected the suggestion because of the war.

Stalin's rejection was influenced by his secret negotiations with the Germans during 1943 over an agreement to end the war. He wanted the Russo-German frontiers of 1914, Russian control over the Straits of the Dardanelles, a free hand for Russia in Asia, and closer economic ties with Germany. Stalin did not agree to a meeting with Churchill and Roosevelt until after Hitler had finally rejected his proposals in September, 1943.[9] The Soviet ruler may have deliberately opened peace negotiations with Hitler hoping that rumors of his disloyalty might frighten the West into dispatching more aid to Russia and hastening the opening of a second front.

On September 4, Roosevelt proposed a meeting in North Africa between November 15 and December 15. The timing suited Stalin, who suggested Teheran as the meeting place. Roosevelt was reluctant to travel that far because of the constitutional requirement to sign bills within ten days of passage. The Taurus Mountains, near Teheran, were often closed in, and this would mean difficult flying weather for planes carrying documents for Roosevelt's signature.

Stalin refused to budge although Roosevelt proposed Basra, Cairo, Asmara, Bagdad, or any port in the eastern Mediterranean. Churchill suggested Beirut, Cyprus, or a ship in the Mediterranean. At last Roosevelt capitulated on November 6 and accepted Teheran. If documents required his signature, he would fly to Tunis, meet the courier, and then return to Teheran.[10]

In preparing for the Teheran Conference, Roosevelt feared that side remarks between Churchill and himself might lead

[9] Peter Kleist, *Zwischen Hitler und Stalin*, 241, 244–47, 260–61, 265–66, 269; Wolfgang Leonhard, *Child of the Revolution*, 255–58.

[10] Roosevelt to Stalin, September 4, 9, October 4, 14, November 8, 1943, *Teheran*, 23–24, 27, 31–32, 71–72; Stalin to Roosevelt, September 8, 12, October 19, November 5, 1943, *ibid.*, 23–24, 25, 33–34, 67–68; Harriman to Roosevelt, October 26, 1943, *ibid.*, 43–44; Hull to Roosevelt, October 26, 1943, *ibid.*, 43–44; Hull to Roosevelt, October 29, 1943, *ibid.*, 45–46.

Stalin to think that they were ganging up on him. Roosevelt dreaded a sudden, bitter, irrelevant question asked by Stalin to provoke argument. He expected Stalin to ask about the Negro problem in the United States, giving names, dates, and places, and number of people involved in lynchings in the South. "Finally," Roosevelt told an aide, "the Marshal might involve my wife in this discussion of our Negro problem. That would make me furious." From his aides, Roosevelt requested information of the Soviet minority problems as ammunition against Stalin. At the same time the President asked for information on the Soviet conservation projects with which to compliment Stalin.[11]

From November 22–26, Roosevelt and Churchill stopped for a meeting at Cairo with Generalissimo Chiang Kai-shek on their way to Teheran. Chiang and his glamorous wife pressed their case for more help in every way possible. The records of this conference are so few and fragmentary that no definite picture can be obtained of the negotiations. The three leaders seem to have had only one plenary meeting, and it was devoted to arguing the merits of a land campaign in Burma with a naval operation at the same time to secure the Andaman Islands.

The conference reached no clear-cut decision. Roosevelt could not help promising Chiang that there would be some future operation in the Bay of Bengal. Churchill rejected Chiang's request for an amphibious operation at the same time as the Burma campaign.

At the close of the conference, the trio issued an important communiqué dealing with the future of the Japanese Empire. Chiang, Roosevelt, and Churchill pledged to strip Japan of all her empire, including territories taken from China and Russia. Korea would become a free and independent nation. By this policy they would create a political vacuum into which they

[11] Henry Field, "How FDR did his Homework," *Saturday Review of Literature*, Vol. XL (July 8, 1961), 8–10.

expected China to move. They could not foresee that a Communist China would one day seek to fill this vacuum.

As the Teheran meeting drew near, there was no accord between Roosevelt and Churchill over their coming encounter with Stalin. Despite one meeting with their generals at Cairo, they do not seem to have found any agreed way to approach him. They could only affirm that operation Overlord [invasion of the European continent through western France] "remained the top of the bill," in the words of Churchill.

Shortly after his arrival in Teheran in the afternoon of November 27, Roosevelt was advised that Stalin and Churchill preferred that he stay at the Russian embassy instead of the American legation. Any visits by Stalin and Churchill and Roosevelt's return calls would necessitate long journeys through narrow streets that would have delighted an assassin. The Soviets had heard rumors of an attempt to assassinate some of the leaders during the conference. Churchill could live at the British legation because of its proximity to the Russian embassy.

Roosevelt did not believe there was any plot, but he was convinced that Stalin wanted him to live at the Russian embassy. Because Roosevelt had come to Teheran determined to like Stalin and make himself liked, he accepted the Russian offer.[12] A well-protected caravan drove to the Russian embassy from the American legation, but Roosevelt, Harry Hopkins, Admiral William D. Leahy, chief of staff to Roosevelt, and a Secret Service man drove so swiftly through the side streets that they reached the embassy before the diversional caravan. Within the confines of the Russian embassy and the British legation, surrounded by British troops, NKVD, and Secret Service agents, the trio commenced their deliberations.

[12] Frances Perkins, *The Roosevelt I Knew,* 83.

6

Teheran, 1943

$\mathbb{R}$oosevelt began his first summit conference with a private meeting with Stalin on November 28. "I am glad to see you," he said as Stalin entered the President's quarters, "I have tried for a long time to bring this about." Stalin admitted that he had been partly responsible for the delay in the meeting.

Roosevelt asked about the conditions on the eastern front. After Stalin explained the battle situation, the President bewailed his lack of power to achieve the removal of thirty or forty German divisions from the Russian front. Roosevelt intimated that he would like to transfer some of the British and American merchant fleet to Russian use after the war. Stalin offered raw materials for the United State's use in return for the ships. The discussion turned briefly to Chiang Kai-shek, the war in China, then to Lebanon, the Free French, and their leader, Charles de Gaulle.

Stalin complained that De Gaulle did not represent physical France and that France should be punished after the war. Roosevelt agreed, declaring that "in the future, no Frenchman over 40, and particularly no Frenchman who had ever taken part in the French government, should be allowed to return to position in the future." Nor did he think that France would quickly be re-established as a strong nation. First he would have the French citizens "become honest citizens." Stalin added that no Allied blood should be shed to restore Indochina to the old French colonial rule. "The French," he insisted, "must pay for their criminal collaboration with Germany." Roosevelt was in full agreement. While damning the French, both leaders chose to overlook Stalin's eager collaboration with Hitler from 1939 to 1941.

Roosevelt confessed that it was best not to discuss the question of India with Churchill because he "had no solution of that question." In the future he would discuss the question with Stalin. Roosevelt "felt that the best solution would be reform from the bottom, somewhat on the Soviet line." Stalin observed that such reform would bring on revolution. As they left to join Churchill, Roosevelt declared how glad he was for the opportunity to meet Stalin in "informal and different circumstances."[1]

In the conference room of the Soviet embassy, the three leaders met with their staffs at 4:00 P.M. on November 28. The meeting represented "the greatest concentration of power that the world had ever seen," Churchill observed. Roosevelt took the chair, announcing that they would talk, "with complete frankness on all sides with nothing that was said to be made public." He was confident of the success of the meeting and that the three nations would not only co-operate in prosecuting the war, but would "also remain in close touch for generations to come."

[1] Roosevelt-Stalin meeting, November 28, 1943, *Teheran*, 482–86.

Roosevelt then launched into an explanation of the campaign in the Pacific, stressing American efforts to keep China in the war. Turning to Europe, he explained that difficulties in sea transport had prevented setting a date for a cross-channel invasion. At the recent Quebec meeting, Churchill and he had agreed on an expedition about May 1, 1944. There were some unresolved questions on the use of Allied forces in the Mediterranean.

Stalin was happy to hear of the successes against the Japanese. He promised that once Germany had been conquered, he would reinforce his troops in Siberia and then join in the defeat of Japan. The Marshal reviewed operations on the eastern front against the Germans. Italy was ill suited as a base for launching an attack on Germany, according to Stalin. His military leaders believed that Hitler sought to keep as many Allied divisions in Italy as possible. Germany should be attacked through northern France. Even if the Balkans were opened up, the heart of Germany was still far away. "Northern France was still the best," Stalin declared. Thus he threw his support wholly behind the ideas of the American chiefs of staff, much to their delight.

Prime Minister Churchill opened with a statement on the African and Italian campaigns as clearly secondary but the best that could be done in 1943. With the fall of Rome, probably by January 1, 1944, troops would be available for use in southern France or across the Adriatic in support of the Yugoslavs. "There was no plan to send a large army to the Balkans," Churchill declared.

The possibility of bringing Turkey into the war interested Churchill because then the Aegean Sea could be opened to the Allies, German control of Greece would be threatened, and the route to Russia would be shortened. Roosevelt supported the idea of forces sent to support Tito and then to turn northeast into Rumania, there joining forces with the advancing Russians. Churchill asked for Stalin's opinion on these matters.

The Soviet dictator, interested only in the invasion of France (code name "Overlord"), maintained that the dispersal of Allied troops in the Mediterranean would not aid Overlord except for an invasion of southern France. He would have this come two months before Overlord to draw troops away from the north. Stalin did not believe that Turkey would enter the war.

According to Stalin, Russian experience had shown the need to launch an offensive from two sides. Such an attack, he thought, would be successful in France. Churchill returned to the question of Turkish entrance into the war, but neither Roosevelt nor Stalin gave him encouragement. The first meeting of the leaders ended.[2]

An argument in favor of the summit conference alleges that such meetings give an opportunity for private talks in the relaxed atmosphere of cocktails and dinner. The first of these came the evening of November 28 when Roosevelt was host to Stalin and Churchill at dinner in his quarters.

Stalin introduced the question of France, arguing that France did not deserve special treatment and "had no right to retain her empire." Nor would he have France play an important role in the postwar world. French rulers were rotten and ought to be punished for their criminal collaboration with Germany. He condemned them for surrendering France to Germany. After the war no important strategic bases should be left in the hands of France. Roosevelt concurred in part, but only Churchill attempted to defend France, voicing his hope in a "flourishing and lively France." Stalin would not allow any significant role for France in the postwar world. France would be only "a charming and pleasant country," nothing more. General Charles de Gaulle, leader of the Free French forces, was of no importance to Stalin.

The conversation turned to Germany. Stalin swore that Germany must be so weak that never again could she plunge the world into war. But when Churchill suggested measures to disarm Germany, Stalin found them all inadequate. He had no faith in the reformation of the German people. As for Hitler, he

[2] Plenary meeting, November 28, 1943, *ibid.*, 487–508.

thought him a "very able man but not basically intelligent, lacking in culture and with a primitive approach to political and other problems." Unlike Roosevelt, who believed that Hitler was mentally unbalanced, the Soviet marshal considered him sane because otherwise he could not have accomplished the unification of the German people.

For the first time the question of Poland came up—the issue that had precipitated the war. Stalin announced that he would like the Poles to have the Oder River for their frontier.

Roosevelt mentioned international control of the approaches to the Baltic Sea. Stalin misunderstood the translation and thought the President was proposing international control over the Baltic States, an area Stalin coveted. He declared: "The Baltic states had by an expression of the will of the people voted to join the Soviet Union and [that] this question was not therefore one for discussion."[3]

After Roosevelt had gone to bed, Churchill continued the conversation with Stalin. The Premier feared that Germany would swiftly recover from the war and start a new one within fifteen to twenty years. Churchill insisted that they must make the world safe from Germany for the next fifty years.

Stalin wanted restraints on German industrial capacity lest it revive too quickly. He warned Churchill of the German watchmakers and furniture factories that could make shells and toy rifles to train Germans to shoot. Churchill argued that Britain, Russia, and the United States must learn from their past mistakes and control, dismember, and supervise Germany. Within a generation, he hoped, the German people could be re-educated. But Stalin inclined towards pessimism.

Churchill stressed the British intention to re-establish a strong, independent Poland without any pledge to specific Polish frontiers. Soviet considerations of security should be the determining factor. Stalin reaffirmed his intention of making the Oder River the western frontier of Poland. Churchill wanted the

[3] Dinner meeting, November 28, 1943, *ibid.*, 509–14.

Polish frontier moved westward at German expense, but he was without authority from Parliament to draw frontier lines. He thought Roosevelt was in a similar predicament, but he wanted some policy agreed on at Teheran to recommend to the Poles. Stalin insisted that he did not want Poland, but he would be satisfied with some German land. On that note they parted for the evening.[4]

Churchill asked for a private meeting with Roosevelt on the morning of November 29, but the President refused because he wanted to avoid private meetings which might arouse Russian suspicions. Instead, Roosevelt continued to meet with Stalin without any concert of tactics and ideas with Churchill.[5]

Stalin and Roosevelt met in the afternoon of November 29 for a private talk with only their interpreters present. Roosevelt presented his idea on the future United Nations. He suggested a world-wide body of the members of the United Nations to meet periodically and to suggest measures to a smaller body. This would be an executive committee composed of the Soviet Union, the United States, Great Britain, China, two European nations, a South American nation, one nation each from the Middle East, the Far East, and the British Commonwealth. The executive committee would handle all nonmilitary matters. Roosevelt confessed that he doubted if the United States Congress would be bound by this body. "The Four Policemen," composed of the United States, China, Russia, and Great Britain, would deal with any emergency or threat to the peace. With this quartet, Roosevelt hoped to avoid the delay and procrastination which cursed the League of Nations.

Stalin observed that China might be resented by European nations when she played the role of policeman. As an alternative, the Marshal proposed regional committees. Roosevelt admitted that Churchill had advocated three regional committees dealing with Europe, the Far East, and the Americas. Churchill wanted

[4] Winston S. Churchill, *Closing the Ring,* 359–62.
[5] Robert E. Sherwood, *Roosevelt and Hopkins,* 784.

the United States on the European committee, but Roosevelt confessed to Stalin his reluctance to consider a European committee with the United States as a member lest Congress refuse to dispatch troops to Europe. Stalin reminded him that the duties of "the Four Policemen" might require the dispatch of American soldiers to Europe. Roosevelt planned that the United States would only send planes and ships; Britain and Russia would send the soldiers.

The President proposed two methods to deal with the threats to peace. A quarantine could be imposed on a small country. If that method was insufficient, the "Four Policemen" could issue an ultimatum, and, if there were a refusal, bombard and invade.

Stalin feared German recovery within twenty years, and Roosevelt's proposed organization lacked the strength to prevent this development. To prevent a German revival, Stalin advocated the control of strong points along the German frontiers. For Japan, he proposed a similar method; Roosevelt agreed.

Stalin was cool to Chinese participation in the "Four Policemen," but Roosevelt countered that he had been thinking of the future. It was better to have a nation of 400 million Chinese as friends than as potential troublemakers. The meeting ended with the President arguing that the policemen would keep track of any German attempts to convert factories to the manufacture of munitions. He would have strategic positions in the world placed at the disposal of world organizations to prevent future German and Japanese aggression.[6]

In the afternoon of November 29, the three leaders once more assembled for a plenary meeting with the British and American military advisers. Stalin had only Marshal K. E. Voroshilov and V. M. Molotov, his foreign minister.

General Alan Brooke, chief of the imperial general staff, and General George Marshall, United States Army chief of staff, reported on the morning meeting of the military staff. Suddenly

[6] Roosevelt-Stalin meeting, November 29, 1943, *Teheran*, 529–33.

Stalin asked who would command Overlord, but Roosevelt replied that the commander had not yet been chosen. Although he did not request a veto over the selection of a commander, Stalin insisted that the appointment should come quickly. Probably he hoped that after the appointment, Anglo-American planning for the second front would proceed with greater speed.

Churchill returned to his query over the Mediterranean operations. He complained of the troops which would be idle in the Mediterranean theater. The Conference should consider ways to make full use of these troops and give the fullest aid to Overlord. Landing craft for two divisions allotted to British forces in the Mediterranean could be put to use and thus aid Overlord by pinning down German forces. Operations could be launched in central Italy. Rhodes could be taken if Turkey entered the war, and the force could be used in southern France in conjunction with Overlord.

The Prime Minister wanted more study of the problem of increased aid to Tito and his forces. This was imperative because there were twenty-one German divisions and twenty-one Bulgarian divisions in the Balkans. Churchill assured Stalin that Great Britain had no ambitions in the Balkans, but merely wanted to keep the Germans from sending these troops to repulse Overlord. Last of all there was Turkey. If they could bring her to declare war on Germany, German morale would suffer, and Bulgaria, Rumania, and Hungary would all be affected.

Stalin did not expect Turkey to enter the war, but if that occurred, Russia would take care of Bulgaria. To him Yugoslavia was unimportant, and he was uninterested in the entry of Turkey into the war and the occupation of Rhodes. The only important military problem was Overlord. "Nothing should be done," he declared, "to distract attention from that operation." The date for Overlord must be set, there should be an invasion of southern France, and the commander-in-chief for Overlord should be appointed as soon as possible.

Roosevelt expressed interest in a discussion of the other

projects, but he supported Stalin by insisting that nothing should upset the timing of Overlord. The Yugoslavs should be helped and German divisions contained, but not on such a scale that Overlord would have to be postponed. To which Stalin commented, "You are right! You are right!"

Once more Churchill rehearsed his arguments, while Stalin continually interrupted. He emphasized British reluctance to mount Overlord unless certain that German strength in the Low Countries and France would be limited to twelve first-line and fifteen reserve divisions. The Prime Minister did not want British forces to stand idle. Stalin sneered: "It looked as though Mr. Churchill thought that the Russians were suggesting that the British armies do nothing." Churchill ignored him. If they slackened their efforts in Italy, German troops could then be transferred to France to meet the invading armies. Operations in the eastern Mediterranean would contain German troops and aid Overlord.

Stalin broke in, "What if there are 13 divisions, not 12?" Again Churchill ignored him and commented on the possibilities for action if Turkey entered the war. Roosevelt wanted the chiefs of staff to consider the problems of Overlord and the Mediterranean. Stalin objected, "We chiefs of state have more power and more authority than a committee." They only needed to select the commander of Overlord, choose the date, and arrange for operations in the south of France. Because Roosevelt insisted, Stalin stopped objecting. He turned on Churchill and asked if the British sincerely believed in Overlord or merely said so to reassure Russia. Churchill retorted that, if the conditions were as agreed on in the Moscow Conference, Great Britain would "hurl every scrap of strength across the channel."

Despite Stalin's objections, the meeting ended with a decision for the military staffs to meet, and the foreign secretaries and Harry Hopkins to confer separately.[7]

To Stalin that afternoon, Churchill may have seemed a ro-

[7] Plenary meeting, November 29, 1943, *ibid.*, 533–52.

tund British capitalist who wanted Soviet soldiers to fight and die while Overlord was postponed. Churchill and his officers dreaded another Dunkirk if they met unforeseen resistance from the Germans on the beaches of France. Of the three leaders, only Churchill had fought in the trenches during World War I when an entire generation of British manhood had almost been obliterated. Britain could not endure another blood bath. He wanted the invasion only under the most favorable circumstances, but he did not dare reveal his fears to Stalin. Churchill was not seeking to extend political power into the Balkans as Roosevelt imagined. His only thought was to defeat Germany without another wholesale slaughter of British youth.

That evening Stalin was the host at dinner. He taunted Churchill because of his dogged argument during the afternoon. The experience of meeting such stout opposition was new to Stalin. Again and again he inferred that Churchill "nursed a secret affection for Germany and desired to see a soft peace." Stalin advocated that perhaps 100,000 of the German general staff be liquidated; Churchill spoke up against "the cold blooded execution of soldiers who had fought for their country." Certainly war criminals must stand trial for their crimes, but "I would rather be taken out into the garden here and now and be shot myself than sully my own and my country's honor by such infamy." Enjoying what seemed to him a joke, Roosevelt suggested a compromise by shooting 49,000. Thinking himself wise beyond his years, Elliott Roosevelt, the President's son who accompanied his father to Teheran, arose and announced that Stalin was right and that it did not make much difference in any event.

Despite signs from his foreign secretary, Anthony Eden, that Roosevelt and Stalin were not serious, Churchill left the dinner. He would not return until Stalin personally assured him it was a joke.

The dinner meeting of the leaders was notable for two admissions from Stalin: the Soviet army had been badly organized and fought poorly against the Finns, and when the Germans attacked in 1941, the Red Army was not a first-class fighting force.

Stalin and Roosevelt agreed that strategic strong points should be held by the Allies to stop Germany and Japan. Churchill announced that Britain would join the occupation forces, but only if invited. Britain did not want any additional territory, he declared. Whatever territory Britain released would be done of her own volition.

Stalin favored increases in the British Empire in the vicinity of Gibralter. He suggested that the United States and Britain should install more friendly governments in Spain and Portugal. When Churchill asked about Soviet territorial desires, the Marshal replied: "There is no need to speak at the present time about any Soviet desires, but when the time comes, we will speak."[8]

Disturbed by the treatment Roosevelt gave him regarding a private meeting, Churchill sought out Stalin on November 30 to explain his position on Overlord. He wanted to dispose of any idea that Stalin might have that "Churchill and the British staffs mean to stop Overlord if they can, because they want to invade the Balkans instead." Churchill pleaded that he had only resisted a proposed American operation in the Bay of Bengal which would drain off much needed landing craft. These craft could transport British forces for operations in the Mediterranean area, which would draw German troops away from the scene of Overlord. Churchill wanted the Americans to detach some ships from the Pacific, "but the American were very touchy about the Pacific."

The Prime Minister explained British preparations for Overlord and the coming campaigns in Italy as evidence of British sincerity. Stalin commented that the Russian army was greatly dependent on the invasion of France; without it, morale would suffer badly. Once he knew the date for Overlord, Stalin prom-

---

[8] Dinner meeting, November 29, 1943, *ibid.*, 552–55; Churchill, *Closing the Ring,* 373–74.

At the Teheran Conference in 1943, President Franklin D. Roosevelt and Winston Churchill, hoping to ensure the defeat of Adolf Hitler, permitted Marshal Joseph Stalin to invade Eastern Europe. Seated from left to right on the porch of the Russian Embassy at Teheran, Iran, are Joseph Stalin, Franklin D. Roosevelt, and Winston Churchill.

Courtesy Wide World Photos

The Yalta Conference in 1945 reinforced the Russian gains made at Teheran. Seated from left to right are Winston Churchill, Franklin D. Roosevelt, and Joseph Stalin; the American army officer wearing the fur collar is General George C. Marshall.

ised heavy blows. Churchill thought they would know by lunchtime.[9]

On November 30 at a luncheon meeting of the three leaders and their interpreters, Roosevelt read to his colleagues the recommendations of the combined British and American staffs. The attack in Italy would continue until the line Pisa-Rimini; there would be an invasion of southern France about the same time as Overlord, the latter to be launched during May, 1944. Stalin was delighted and promised the help of the Red Army.

Later the conversation turned to political matters. Stalin favored the independence of Korea and the return to China of Manchuria, Formosa, and the Pescadores Islands. Churchill and Roosevelt were agreeable.

Stalin mentioned the size of Russia as a help in saving her from Germany. Churchill was favorable to access for Russia to warmwater ports. Since Churchill had raised the question of access, Stalin wanted to know if the Montreux Convention, which governed the Straits of the Dardanelles, could not be relaxed. Churchill was sympathetic but would not touch the matter for the present.

Roosevelt returned to his idea of a type of Hanseatic League for the Baltic Sea and international control over the Kiel Canal. Stalin conceded the value of these ideas, but he wanted to know what would be done for Russia in the Far East. Neither Roosevelt nor Churchill hastened to offer large pieces of territory to Stalin, although Roosevelt suggested Dairen as a free port open to Russia. Stalin believed the Chinese might not be agreeable; Roosevelt countered that he was thinking in terms of a free port with an international guarantee.

Churchill ended the luncheon with the observation that the nations who governed the world after the war must be satisfied in their territorial ambitions in order that the world might be at peace.[10]

[9] Ibid., 378.
[10] Luncheon meeting, November 30, 1943, Teheran, 565–68.

At the plenary meeting on November 30, General Brooke reported that the military leaders had agreed on launching Overlord during the month of May, 1944, and landing as large a force as possible about the same time in southern France. To keep the military squeeze on Germany, Churchill promised to inform the Soviet armies of all Anglo-American plans. Stalin failed to reciprocate with a promise to divulge Russian plans. However, he pledged to launch simultaneously an offensive from the east sufficient enough to pin down German troops and prevent their transfer to France. Roosevelt echoed Churchill's call for co-ordination of the military staffs in their planning. Again Stalin was silent. The President promised to appoint the commander-in-chief of Overlord within a few days after consultation with Churchill.

The evening of November 30 saw a jolly celebration of Churchill's birthday in the British legation, which had first been thoroughly searched by Russian agents. Good humor and a multitude of toasts to one and all made the evening memorable to Churchill. The road had been long and bloody since those grim days in May, 1940, when he assumed the office of King's first minister amid defeat. Then the United States had been neutral and Russia had been allied to Nazi Germany. Now the leaders of both nations sat on either side of him as his wartime allies.

In the numerous toasts little was said of political significance. Stalin hailed Roosevelt and Churchill as "fighting friends," but unable to resist a dig at Churchill, he added "if it is possible for me to consider Mr. Churchill my friend." He praised Roosevelt for his defense of the weak and helpless and for his aid to democracy. Churchill admired the President's courageous action in 1933 which "prevented a revolution in the United States." In a toast to Stalin, Churchill hailed him as a great figure of Russian history worthy of the title "Stalin the Great."

Before the toasting ended, Stalin paid tribute to American industry, for without the planes produced by the United States the war would have been lost. Stalin gave thanks to Roosevelt and the American people for developing such productive capacity and for achieving the delivery of these machines to Russia. He added, "Without the use of those machines, through Lend-Lease, we would lose this war." Thus did the leader of world Communism thank the President of capitalist United States.

Roosevelt spoke the final words.

We have different customs and philosophies and ways of life. Each of us works out our scheme of things according to the desires and ideas of our own peoples. But we have proved here at Teheran that the varying ideals of our nations can come together in a harmonious whole, moving unitedly for the common good of ourselves and of the world. So we leave this historic gathering, we can see in the sky, for the first time, that traditional symbol of hope, the rainbow.[11]

On December 1, a luncheon conference of the three leaders and their foreign-affairs advisers was devoted to Churchill's exposition of the approach to be made to involve Turkey in the war. Harry Hopkins and Roosevelt tried to dampen his enthusiasm by warning that no landing craft would be available for any expedition to help Turkey. Stalin said little, preferring to let the democratic leaders argue.

Roosevelt switched the conversation to Finland, asking Stalin's views. The Marshal declared that he had no designs on Finland if her behavior was proper, and he was ready to negotiate if the Finns proposed suitable conditions. So far their proposals were unsatisfactory. Churchill hoped that nothing would impair Finland's independence and that the reparations would be light. Stalin was not so minded: the Finns must pay in timber, paper, and assorted materials for five to eight years. Frontiers based on the treaty of March 12, 1940, must be re-established. Finland must pay 50 per cent of the damage caused to the U.S.S.R. and expel the Germans.[12]

That afternoon, Stalin and Roosevelt met for their last pri-

[11] Dinner meeting, November 30, 1943, *ibid.*, 469, 582–85, 837.
[12] Luncheon meeting, December 1, 1943, *ibid.*, 585–93.

vate meeting of the conference. Roosevelt admitted that he wanted to discuss matters relating to internal American politics. The following year, 1944, would be an election year, and he would have to consider the votes of six to seven million Americans of Polish extraction. Although he favored moving the Polish frontier to the Oder River, for political reasons he did not want to participate in decisions on the Polish frontier at Teheran or during the coming year. Stalin was sympathetic.

Roosevelt also had voters of Lithuanian, Estonian, and Latvian origins, but he would not go to war with Russia when Stalin's troops reoccupied the Baltic states. The important issue in the United States was the problem of referendum and the right of self-determination. Public opinion would desire expression of the will of these people at some future date. "He personally was confident that the people would vote to join the Soviet Union."

Stalin claimed that he did not know anyone who had raised the question of public opinion when the czar ruled these lands, and he could not see why it was being raised now. There would be opportunity for the expression of the people's will in accordance with the Soviet constitution. He rejected any form of international control.

Roosevelt, mindful of the voters, begged for some public declaration about future elections. Stalin would only repeat that the people would have opportunities in accord with the Soviet constitution.

Roosevelt explained that he felt it "premature" to discuss the proposed world organization now with Churchill. Additional study would be required. Stalin announced his agreement with the President's desire that the organization should be worldwide instead of regional. Probably he changed his mind when he realized that Soviet influence would be greater in a world organization instead of one that was regional.[13]

[13] Roosevelt-Stalin meeting, December 1, 1943, *ibid.*, 594–96.

The final meeting of the leaders and their advisers came the same evening. Roosevelt opened with the announcement that the Polish question and the treatment of Germany would be the topics for discussion. Before anyone could advance any ideas, Molotov wanted to know if Russia would get any of the Italian ships. The Prime Minister and the President quickly assented to the delivery to Russia of Italian ships in January, 1944.

Roosevelt brought the conversation back to Poland; he hoped that relations could be re-established between the Polish government-in-exile and the Soviet government. Stalin complained that the Polish government-in-exile was "closely connected with the Germans and their agents in Poland were killing partisans." He had broken off relations with the Polish government-in-exile because they had joined in "slanderous propaganda with the Nazis." If the government-in-exile would end its connection with German agents in Poland and urge the Polish people to fight Germans, Russia would be prepared to negotiate.

Churchill asked about the Russo-Polish frontier, hoping for some formula to present to the Polish government-in-exile whose headquarters were in London. Stalin considered the frontier of 1939 "just and right." Anthony Eden, the British foreign secretary, observed that this was the "Ribbentrop-Molotov line" which had originated in the Nazi-Soviet Pact of August 23, 1939. Ignoring the jibe at his pact with Hitler, Stalin declared that he was uninterested in the name, but he would not permit the Poles to hold the Ukraine and White Russia which they had acquired in 1920 when the Soviet Union was weak. Molotov chimed in with the announcement that this was really the "Curzon line" which had been suggested in 1920 but rejected by the Polish government.

A map was produced which Stalin consulted with interest, marking the region in red which he wanted returned to Russia. He complained that the map was in error because Polish statistics had been used. At Churchill's insistence, Stalin agreed to the Curzon Line as the Russo-Polish frontier, except for an area in northern East Prussia.

When the conferees turned to Germany, Roosevelt proposed that Germany be broken up into five self-governing areas, with the Kiel Canal, Hamburg, the Ruhr, and the Saar all under international control. Churchill wanted Prussia separated from Germany, with the Palatinate and south Germany joined in a "confederation of the Danube." Stalin was uninterested in such details.

He advocated a thorough dismembering of Germany, not merely breaking it up into a few states as Roosevelt suggested. Stalin feared a confederation of German states because it would provide the foundation to rebuild a larger Germany. As for the individual Germans, they all seemed the same: "all German soldiers fought like devils." The Prussian officer corps had to be eliminated. Because there would always be a strong urge to unite Germany, Stalin wanted an international organization to preserve peace by neutralizing this tendency. Every means must be used, including force. "The victorious nations must have the strength to beat the Germans if they ever start on the path of a new war."

Churchill asked if "Stalin contemplated a Europe composed of little states, disjointed, separated, and weak." Stalin replied, "Not Europe, but Germany." Roosevelt offered no objection and by his silence appeared to approve.

Churchill was not in full accord with Stalin, pointing out that the parts of Germany would inevitably unite unless they were combined in larger units to offset the attraction of a greater Germany. Then the Prime Minister returned to the Polish question, seeking a formula on the frontier to present to the Poles in London. Poland would have the Curzon Line and the Oder River as frontiers together with part of East Prussia. Stalin agreed, providing Russia could have northern East Prussia. Then he would accept the Curzon Line as the frontier for Russia and Poland.[14]

Later in the same evening, Roosevelt, Stalin, and Churchill drew up the final communiqué and a declaration on Iran. The three powers promised economic aid to Iran while maintaining the nation's independence and territorial integrity.

The trio initialed a secret military agreement that was not released to the public until 1947. The Yugoslav partisans would be aided by every means. Entrance of Turkey into the war was considered most desirable, and if this occurred and Bulgaria attacked Turkey, Soviet Russia would go to war. Overlord would be launched during May, 1944, in conjunction with an invasion through southern France. Soviet forces would attack at the same time from the east to prevent German forces being transferred to France. The three military staffs would keep in close touch regarding future operations and devise cover operations to mislead the enemy.[15]

The next day they went their separate ways: Stalin to Russia, Roosevelt and Churchill back to Cairo for more discussions with their generals over the conduct of the war.

The Teheran Conference was the most important meeting of those held during the war, including Yalta and Potsdam. By agreeing to the plan for Overlord, with Russian forces coming from the east, Roosevelt, Churchill and Stalin had shaped the future of Europe. Regardless of future conferences and agreements, Russian armies would control Eastern Europe and the other allies the West. Russian armies would pass over lands once held or coveted by the czars.

Roosevelt did not see the potential dangers for he was transfixed by the threat of Churchill seeking to push an invasion army into the Balkans and thereby frightening Stalin. Roosevelt would not support Churchill in protecting "real or fancied British in-

14 Political meeting, December 1, 1943, *ibid.*, 596–604.
15 *Ibid.*, 652.

75

terests on the European continent." He was supported in his feelings by his generals and admirals who also still fought the American Revolution. Roosevelt was blind to Churchill's basic argument that everything should be done to tie up as many German troops as possible lest they meet the Allied landing craft when they struck the French beaches.

For Roosevelt this conference was an opportunity to clear up past misunderstandings with Stalin and to end the Russian's suspicions. Roosevelt thought he should strive to stop any wrangling between Churchill and Stalin and act as a mediator. This thought led him to avoid challenging Stalin, if that thought ever entered his mind. Roosevelt believed he had succeeded in showing Stalin that the United States and Great Britain were not united in opposition to Soviet Russia.

The drive of Russia into Central and Eastern Europe did not trouble Roosevelt because he was convinced that only a massive drive through France and into Germany would shorten the war and save American lives. If such a campaign left Russia in control of Eastern Europe, Roosevelt would not worry; winning the war was of greater importance.[16]

Roosevelt was determined to establish as personal a relationship as he could with Stalin in order to overcome his suspicions. For the first three days, Roosevelt felt that he was getting nowhere. Stalin was still "correct, stiff, solemn, not smiling, nothing to get hold of." If the trip was to be devoted solely to paper work, Roosevelt saw no value in it.

Perhaps Stalin might become friendlier if Roosevelt and Churchill were not too close. Roosevelt refused to confer privately with Churchill during the conference. The President intentionally teased Churchill. To Stalin he whispered: "Winston is cranky this morning; he got up on the wrong side of the bed." Then Roosevelt teased him about his cigars, British attitudes, and habits. Stalin broke into a smile. Roosevelt continued until Stalin was laughing and Churchill scowling. Although Churchill

16 Elliott Roosevelt, *As He Saw It*, 175–207.

was supposed to have been warned beforehand, he did not receive Roosevelt's remarks as a joke. The President persisted until it ceased to be funny. Later Roosevelt claimed that teasing Churchill made his relations with Stalin more personal.[17]

Nowhere do the records reveal any indication that Stalin's suspicions of the western Allies were quieted by Roosevelt baiting Churchill. How could one man calm the suspicions of a dictator who suspected everyone in the Soviet Union?

There are no signs indicating that Roosevelt established an intimate relationship with Stalin by taunting Churchill. Yet Roosevelt left Teheran believing that he had somehow gotten through to Stalin. Because he assured Stalin that Russian demands would be met, in the postwar world the Russians would co-operate and work for peace.[18]

Although Roosevelt had not agreed to any secret deal, he had concurred in an important decision which would have incalculable political consequences. When American statesmen met at later summit conferences, the results of the Teheran Conference would influence their labors.

Churchill could not break with his allies. Britain required help, but only Roosevelt and Stalin could supply the guns and soldiers. His duty required him to endure Roosevelt's teasing and Stalin's taunts for Britain's salvation.

At Teheran, Stalin did not conceal his thoughts on the future of Poland and Germany. He would destroy Germany and keep the loot taken from Poland in 1939. His plans meant that Germany would cease to be a political entity. Without another power to fill the vacuum left by Germany's defeat, Russia could dominate Central Europe as had not been possible since the reign of Czar Nicholas I. Stalin's proposal for an international organization to control the remnants of Nazi Germany would only give Russia a veto over German affairs.

[17] Gunther, *Roosevelt in Retrospect*, 17, 334–37; Perkins, *The Roosevelt I Knew*, 382–83.
[18] Sherwood, *Roosevelt and Hopkins*, 798–99.

Few in occupied Europe, Britain, or the United States in December, 1943, would have disagreed with Stalin's desire not only to crush Germany but also to dismember this enemy. Only Churchill offered objections while Roosevelt either agreed smilingly or kept silent lest he offend the Soviet leader. Stalin taunted Churchill about the German question because he sensed hostility. The President kept his silence lest Stalin imagine that he was collaborating with Churchill.

Roosevelt's conception of a dismembered Germany was more nearly attuned to Stalin's. The President failed to grasp the danger in complete dismemberment of Germany. To Roosevelt was not given the power to foresee the future.

The Teheran Conference was not the time to plan for the future world because victory had yet to be won. Yet the decisions made at Teheran would plague Europe for years to come.

7

Yalta, 1945

I N THE SPRING and summer of 1944 the results of the Teheran meeting were harvested. From the east, Russian armies entered Poland, Hungary, Bulgaria, and Rumania. Anglo-American forces invaded France on the Normandy coasts, and later landed on the southern shores of France. Now a gigantic pincers of men, ships, guns, and planes squeezed the Nazi empire.

The advance of the armies made another top-level meeting necessary. Ahead lay the final assault on Japan, the disposition of Germany, decisions on the reconstruction of Europe, and the planning for an organization to replace the League of Nations. Little had been agreed on relating to German reparations and war criminals. Russian participation in the Pacific campaign had been promised, but dates of entry and the amount of aid that could be expected were still unknown, as well as the exact price for Russian entrance into the war in the Far East.

On July 17, 1944, Roosevelt proposed to Stalin a meeting of the three leaders in the "near future because things are moving so fast and so successfully."[1] The meeting ought to be held between September 10 and 15 in northern Scotland. Stalin refused because of the Russian military operations then in progress in Central Europe. Later when Ambassador Averell Harriman suggested a meeting in November somewhere in the Mediterranean area, Stalin rejected the meeting for reasons of health. Roosevelt was still eager for another meeting because he believed "that the three of us and only the three of us, can find the solution to the still unresolved questions."[2] On October 17, Stalin accepted a proposal from Hopkins, conveyed by Andrei Gromyko, to meet with Churchill and Roosevelt at the end of November in the area of the Black Sea.

The negotiations became entangled in arguments over the proposed meeting place. Because Congress would be in session, Roosevelt wanted to have fast communications. His doctors feared the sanitary conditions in a Black Sea port. Roosevelt suggested a variety of meeting places: Athens, Cyprus, Piraeus, Salonika, Constantinople, or Malta. Churchill advocated Alexandria or Jerusalem.

In November, Roosevelt decided that the meeting should be postponed until after his inauguration in January, 1945, for the new term of office. Then they could travel to Rome, the Riviera, Sicily, or an Adriatic port. The new time suited Stalin, but his doctors forbade a trip of such length. His health was so precarious, he alleged, that he could not go outside Russia. When Roosevelt suggested Yalta, Stalin's health improved: he would come. Churchill likewise accepted but complained that if "we spent ten years on research, we could not have found a worse

[1] Roosevelt to Stalin, July 17, 1944, *Foreign Relations of the United States, The Conferences at Malta and Yalta, 1945* (hereafter cited as *Yalta*), 3.
[2] Roosevelt to Harriman, October 4, 1944, *ibid.*, 3.

place in the world than Yalta." He would survive if he brought enough whisky, which was good for typhus and "deadly on lice which thrive in those parts."[3]

The debate over the time and place of meeting delayed the conference until the balance of power had shifted. Despite Churchill's prodding, the Polish government-in-exile in London failed to reach agreement with Stalin over the government and the frontier. Lest he anger Stalin, Roosevelt refused to intervene in these negotiations. On January 5, 1945, over Roosevelt's objections, Stalin recognized some Polish Communists as the provisional government of Poland. Known as the Lubin Committee, this group provided him with an effective puppet government.

By February, 1945, Russian armies were deep in Central Europe. Soviet forces occupied Rumania, Bulgaria, most of Poland, and had invaded Czechoslovakia, Hungary, and Yugoslavia. Already Russian occupation authorities had begun to establish puppet governments similar to the Lublin Committee, headed by local Communists, and justified by the need to secure rear areas. The British and American armies still remained at the German frontiers recovering from the Battle of the Bulge.

Victory was distant, and the casualty lists swelled. Only a handful of the weaker satellites had capitulated. At secret locations within the United States, scientists toiled on a fearsome weapon, the effects of which were still in the realm of science fiction. Looming before American generals was the awful prospect of a bloody invasion of the Japanese home islands after the final defeat of Germany.

There were only a limited number of Anglo-American discussions before the Yalta Conference. Roosevelt, still obsessed by fears of bruising Russian sensitivities, would allow only a minimum of these meetings and none before the combined chiefs of staff met in Malta, January 30–February 2. There, Secretary of State Edward Stettinius conferred with Foreign Secretary

[3] Hopkins to Roosevelt, January 24, 1945, *ibid.*, 39–40.

Anthony Eden, and they found themselves in general agreement on policies to be pursued at Yalta. Roosevelt met with Churchill on February 2, but available records give no indication that they planned jointly on methods of dealing with Stalin.

Instead of a small conference limited to the three leaders, each brought with him a great retinue, complicating housing and feeding problems. The Anglo-American delegations totaled seven hundred persons, male and female, clerks, generals, cooks, and bodyguards. Originally Roosevelt had suggested taking about thirty-five.

Churchill and his party stayed in a large villa built by an English architect for Prince Vorontsov, who had been a czarist ambassador to the Court of St. James in the nineteenth century. Here at 3:00 P.M. on February 4, Stalin called on the British Prime Minister for a short talk about the war. Stalin was optimistic over prospects for completing the defeat of the German armies. He scorned the German failure to break through the Allied front in the Ardennes in December, 1944, as a "stupid maneuver which had harmed Germany."

Field Marshal Harold Alexander then explained the situation on the Italian front. Stalin surprised Churchill by suggesting that the British leave a holding force in Italy and dispatch their troops to Yugoslavia and Hungary, where they could co-operate with the Russians in the final drive on Vienna. Churchill refrained from accepting the invitation.[4]

For the American delegation, home in Crimea was the Lividia Palace, once the summer palace of the czars. German troops had used the palace during the occupation. When they evacuated the Crimea, the palace was thoroughly looted. The Soviet government, however, succeeded in renovating and refurnishing the palace before the conference opened.

Roosevelt and Stalin met on February 4 at 4:00 P.M. in Roosevelt's quarters in the Lividia Palace. Only V. M. Molotov, and the interpreters, V. K. Pavlov and Charles Bohlen, were

[4] Winston S. Churchill, *Triumph and Tragedy*, 347–49.

present. After the usual exchange of amenities, Roosevelt exclaimed that the German destruction in the Crimea had made him more bloodthirsty towards the Germans. "He hoped that Marshal Stalin would again propose a toast to the execution of 50,000 officers of the German army." Stalin observed that "the Germans were savages and seemed to hate with a sadistic hatred the creative work of human beings."

After discussing the progress of the war, Roosevelt inquired how Stalin had fared with De Gaulle on his recent trip to Russia. The Marshal found De Gaulle unrealistic in his demands for full rights for France, which had made so small a contribution to the war.

Roosevelt hastened to impart to Stalin that "the British for two years have had the idea of artificially building up France into a strong power which would have 200,000 troops on the eastern border of France to hold the line for the period required to assemble a strong British army." According to Roosevelt, "the British were a peculiar people and wished to have their cake and eat it too." Both leaders agreed that the French could have a zone of occupation in Germany but only "out of kindness."[5]

At 5:00 P.M. on the same day, the three Allied leaders held their first plenary meeting in the grand ballroom of the palace. Flanked by advisers and interpreters, they sat around a large circular table. At Stalin's suggestion, Roosevelt opened the meeting. The President proposed that military problems be discussed first. Military reports were presented by General A. I. Antonov for the Russian army and General George Marshall for the Anglo-American forces. Stalin was keenly interested in the strength of the Anglo-American forces in the northern part of their front. Admiral Sir Andrew Cunningham finished the reports with brief comments on submarine warfare.

At their first dinner meeting most of the conversation was general until the last half hour. Stalin insisted that the small powers would not have equal voice with the three great powers

[5] Roosevelt-Stalin meeting, February 4, 1945, *Yalta*, 570–73.

in preserving peace. He would concert with Britain and the United States, but "he would never agree to having any action of any great powers submitted to the judgment of the small powers."[6] Roosevelt and Churchill agreed, but only Churchill reminded them of their responsibility to respect the rights of the smaller nations.

Roosevelt opened the second plenary session in the afternoon of February 5 with the announcement that German political matters ought to be discussed. Stalin immediately pushed for agreement on dismemberment of Germany, but Churchill wanted more study of the problem. He rejected hasty decisions about the fate of eighty million people. Stalin demanded a precise agreement on dismemberment of Germany and publication of this intention. Churchill refused to be tied down to any firm decision on Germany. He alleged that he lacked definite opinions on the subject, an unusual situation for him.

At last Roosevelt broke into the dialogue to announce that he favored dismemberment but wanted the matter referred to the foreign ministers who should draft appropriate plans. Despite Stalin's request for an immediate decision on the principle and details of dismemberment, his two colleagues would not be moved. The problem went to the foreign ministers.

Next came the question of the French zone of occupation. Although Churchill stoutly supported France, Stalin was cool towards French participation in the machinery to control Germany. Churchill felt that France had an important role to play in the history of Europe and would be of great help in handling the Germans. When he mentioned his uncertainty about the Americans' stay in Europe, Roosevelt made the first significant statement of the conference. He doubted if Congress and the nation would allow American troops to stay in Europe longer than two years. Now Churchill became more determined than ever to assign the French a zone and to incorporate them into

[6] Dinner meeting, February 4, 1945, *ibid.*, 589.

the control machinery. He needed an ally from the West to face Russia inside Germany.

Stalin argued that if France were given a zone, she would demand a voice in the control of Germany. This he opposed because other nations would then demand a share in controlling Germany. France had not contributed to victory over Germany but had "opened the gate to the enemy." Stalin wanted Germany controlled "by those who have stood firmly against Germany and have made the greatest sacrifice in bringing victory."

Stalin conveniently overlooked his help to Hitler's conquest of Czechoslovakia, Poland, and France. His colleagues ignored his sins because they still needed his help.

Stalin called on Ivan Maisky, the Russian ambassador in London, to present the Soviet reparations plan. Besides losing 80 per cent of her heavy industry, Germany would make payments in kind for the next ten years. A three-power body would supervise the reparations, with priorities established on the basis of those nations who had contributed the most and suffered the greatest. The Soviet Union was entitled to reparations totaling $10,000,000,000.

Churchill reminded them of the dreary history of reparations after World War I. He doubted that Russia could get this amount; if there were any chance of benefitting from large reparations, he would favor the idea because of the British economic burden.

Roosevelt was willing to support the Soviet claims for reparations, but he would neither starve the Germans nor lend them money as had been done after World War I. He would help the Soviets attain the desired reparations, but the Germans should not "become a burden on the world." Yet he felt the reparations would not meet demands. Thus he had not committed the United States to the utter destruction of the German economy as some in Washington had demanded. He and Stalin accepted Churchill's proposal that the issue be turned over to a commission whose directives would be drafted by the foreign ministers. Stalin, however, reminded his audience that those powers who "had contributed the most to the common victory should be given priority in the matter of reparations." The United States could take over German property within her frontiers as her share. France could state her claims after Belgium, Yugoslavia, and Poland had been satisfied. Churchill argued that "the exertion in the war should [not] be taken into consideration. Remember the saying of each according to his needs."

They agreed to discuss the future world organization, the United Nations, and the Polish question at the next plenary meeting.[7]

On February 6, Stettinius reported that the foreign ministers had agreed on inserting "dismemberment" in the surrender terms for Germany. They failed to agree on reparations and the French role in controlling Germany. Then Stettinius outlined the voting procedure in the Security Council. He announced American approval of the veto power of the big powers. The permanent members of the Security Council could not use the veto in procedural matters nor in cases involving peaceful settlement of disputes to which one of the permanent members was a party.

The State Department had recommended this to Roosevelt as absolutely necessary in order to win the support of the small powers and their supporters in the United States. Without this provision the Big Three might appear to be trying to rule the world.

Churchill had come around to Roosevelt's position on this issue before the Yalta Conference. Stalin had already informed the President of his opposition. Now he asked that any decision be postponed in order to give him time to study the documents. He seemed to feel that Britain and the United States might find a way to swing the United Nations against Russia.

[7] Plenary meeting, February 5, 1945, *ibid.*, 611–33.

The Polish question came up next. Roosevelt supported the Curzon Line with concessions made to Poland in the vicinity of Lvov, a position advanced by the State Department in its briefing book. He also wanted a representative government for Poland composed of all the principal political parties. Poland should continue friendly relations with the Soviet Union.

Churchill accepted the Curzon Line but emphasized that Poland must rule her own house. The frontier was not as vital to him as Polish sovereignty and political independence. "He wanted to see the Poles have a home where they could organize their lives as they wished." His government desired Poland to be "mistress in her own house and captain of her soul."

Stalin launched into a long tirade, insisting that the question of Poland involved Russian security and honor. "Throughout history Poland had been the corridor for attack on Russia." Because of Polish weakness, Germany had attacked Russia twice in thirty years. He could not accept the Curzon Line which had been drawn by foreigners, and he could not give up territory which the great Lenin had refused to yield. The western frontiers of Poland must extend to the Western Neisse River. As to the future government, while there had been some chance of fusion between the Lublin government and the London Poles in the autumn, that was impossible now.

Stalin demanded security for the Russian armies in the rear areas, where Poles were sniping at his soldiers. Agents of the London Poles continued to maintain forbidden radio contact with their headquarters. Russian supply bases had been attacked. He would support the government which would give his army peace behind the front lines. The Lublin government appeared to him the more successful in keeping peace. Roosevelt, who had abstained from the discussion, called for adjournment because of the late hour. Churchill returned to the attack. The Lublin government did not even represent one-third of the Polish nation. He had feared a clash between the Lublin government and the Polish Underground Army. To Churchill, the Lublin government could not claim to represent the Polish nation.

Roosevelt insisted on ending the discussion. He declared: "Poland has been a source of trouble for over five hundred years."

"All the more," Churchill retorted, "must we do what we can to put an end to these troubles."[8]

At the plenary meeting on February 7, Roosevelt turned the discussion again to the Polish question. He too assigned less priority to drawing frontiers than to a new form of government. He had written a letter to Stalin the previous evening asking if Polish delegates from London and Lublin could be summoned to Yalta to confer with the three leaders.[9] Stalin reported that he had not yet been able to contact the Lublin leaders.

Molotov took the floor and, to the delight of the United States delegation, reported his government's acceptance of the voting procedure in the Security Council. To those working on the future United Nations, Stalin's approval of the voting procedures alone made the Yalta conference worthwhile.

Then Moltov proposed that two or three of the Soviet republics be admitted as original members of the United Nations: Ukraine, White Russia, and Lithuania. Molotov based this demand on the sacrifices of these republics and on the evolution of the dominions of the British Commonwealth into independent nations who would become members of the United Nations. To Stettinius, Roosevelt passed a note: "This is not so good."

Although he thanked the Russians for their decision, Roosevelt was reluctant to accept their proposal and perhaps purposely launched into a rambling monologue about the difference in structure and tradition of the United States, Russia, and Great

[8] Plenary meeting, February 6, 1945, *ibid.*, 660–81; Churchill, *Triumph and Tragedy*, 372.

[9] Roosevelt to Stalin, February 6, 1945, *Yalta*, 727–28. Roosevelt was greatly troubled because the three powers could not agree over the Polish question. He wrote: "I hope I do not have to assure you that the United States will never lend its support in any way to any provisional government in Poland that would be inimical to your interests."

Britain. He requested that Molotov's proposal be studied by the foreign ministers, whom he also wanted to consider summoning a conference at the end of March to set up the new world organization.

Churchill was sympathetic towards the Russian proposal. "His heart went out to mighty Russia which though bleeding was beating down the tyrants in her path." But he needed time to discuss the admission of three republics with Eden. The Prime Minister was not eager to commence organizing the United Nations. Churchill objected because the war would still be raging, and the governments in exile would be unable to speak for their people suffering under occupation. Roosevelt insisted that the matter go to the foreign ministers. Churchill agreed but warned that this was not a mere technical decision. Privately Roosevelt dismissed Churchill's objections as influenced by British domestic politics.

The Prime Minister brought up the Iranian problem, suggesting that the matter be turned over to the foreign ministers; his colleagues were agreeable. Roosevelt rambled off on a discourse about the need for trees to make Iran prosperous. The new world organization should survey the needs of impoverished countries in order to help them. On he wandered, suggesting a Tennessee Valley Authority for Europe, but no one pursued any of his ideas.

Molotov then produced Russian proposals on the government and frontiers of Poland. The Russians accepted the Curzon Line as the eastern frontier of Poland. The western frontier would begin at Stettin on the Baltic, then swing south along the Oder and Neisse rivers. Soviet leaders were agreeable to adding "some democratic leaders from Polish émigré circles" to the Lublin government. Allied governments should then recognize this enlarged Polish government. Elections should be held as soon as possible. Molotov, Harriman, and Sir Archibald Clark Kerr should discuss enlarging the Polish government and submit proposals.

Roosevelt had no objection except for the use of the word *"émigré"* in referring to the London Poles, who might be added to the provisional Polish government in Lublin. He wanted to study the proposal with Stettinius. Already Stettinius had slipped a note to Roosevelt warning him about the constitutional question involved in settling a boundary problem.

Churchill objected also to *"émigré,"* and he protested moving the Polish frontiers to the Oder-Neisse Line. The Prime Minister considered it "a pity to stuff the Polish goose so full of German food that it got indigestion." British public opinion would be shocked at the necessity of moving large numbers of Germans. Curtly Stalin declared that most of the German inhabitants had already fled. Churchill requested time to consider the proposal.[10]

In the afternoon of February 8, Roosevelt and Stalin met again privately with a minimum of attendants. Roosevelt asked for air bases on Russian soil for use in the Far East against Japan; Stalin had no objections. Stalin acceded to requests for American use of airfields around Budapest and for permission for United States experts to survey bomb damage in areas occupied by Russian forces.

In answer to the Marshal's plea, Roosevelt promised to seek changes in legislation in order to make shipping available for transfer on credit without interest. The President declared that the British "had never sold anything without commercial interest, but that he had different ideas."[11]

Stalin presented his demands for Japanese territory. These were not unknown to the President because Harriman had reported them on December 15, 1944. Roosevelt did not reject the Soviet claim to the southern half of the Sakhalin and all the Kuril Islands. He preferred that Dairen, in Manchuria, be made a free port under an international commission. Roosevelt would not accept Stalin's claim for use of the Manchurian railroads until after talking with Chiang Kai-shek.

[10] Plenary meeting, February 7, 1945, *ibid.*, 709–26.
[11] Roosevelt-Stalin meeting, February 8, 1945, *ibid.*, 766–71.

Both men regretted inviting the British into Korea, but it was necessary. Both were agreeable to a short trusteeship over Korea; Roosevelt suggested Soviet, American, and Chinese representatives as administrators.

Roosevelt favored a trusteeship over French Indochina although the British were opposed because of reflection on their control of Burma. Roosevelt had no desire to return the country to French rule because, as he contended, "France had done nothing to improve the natives since she had the colony." Stalin raised no objections.

Both men regretted that Chiang Kai-shek did not co-operate more closely with the Chinese Communists. Roosevelt blamed the Kuomintang more than the Communists for the lack of co-operation.

At the plenary meeting of February 8, the foreign ministers reported agreement on calling a United Nations conference over the new world organization on April 25, 1945, in San Francisco. After some quibbling with Stalin over invitations to nations who had no diplomatic relations with Russia, they agreed to invite all nations who had declared war on Germany by March 1, 1945. The San Francisco conference could decide whether to admit two Soviet republics to original membership.

When they returned the conversation to Poland, Roosevelt presented his counter proposals. He accepted the Curzon Line in the east but not the Neisse in the west. A three-member presidential committee should form a Polish provisional government from the leaders in Poland and London. Churchill was willing to accept this proposal.

Molotov took up the battle. He demanded that the Lublin government be enlarged. The present government existed and had great authority; the Polish people had received it enthusiastically. Roosevelt's proposal might create disunity among the Poles. They needed only to discuss "how many and who they should be." This could be done by Molotov, Harriman, Clark Kerr, three Poles from the Communist government, and two from the London Poles. He rejected Roosevelt's proposed presidential committee.

Churchill declared: "We are at the crucial point of this great conference." If they separated while still recognizing two Polish governments, the conference would have failed. He had information that the Lublin government was not supported by the Poles. If the British government endorsed the Lublin government, the exiled Poles would feel betrayed. He had yielded on the frontiers, but if he gave way on the government, his cabinet would be charged with forsaking Poland. If the London government were to be jettisoned, it must be on the basis of universal suffrage and the secret ballot.

Stalin insisted that the Communist Poles were popular because they had not fled from the invader but had stayed and fought in the underground. Now there had been a great change in the attitude of the Poles towards Russia because of the liberation in which the London Poles had no part. The Soviet liberation of Poland had completely altered the Polish attitude. "The old resentment has completely disappeared. Now there is good will toward Russia." The Lublin government was popular because the people saw them while the London Poles were absent. Stalin maintained that they could not ignore the feelings of the Polish people. Personally he favored democratic elections, but until these were held, they had to deal with the provisional government. The Lublin government was no different than De Gaulle's which had not been elected. Was De Gaulle more popular than Boleslaw Bierut, the president of the Lublin government? "We cannot demand more of Poland than of France," Stalin pontificated. The Polish government had even instituted significant reforms. Where were De Gaulle's?

In the argument Stalin had by far the better of the exchange. The comparison with De Gaulle could not be answered. Stalin's insistence on the Lublin government as the base for a new government meant that the Communists' could be considered the more legal government. Accordingly, Poles who were non-Communists could not enter the reconstructed government on the same level as the Communists. They must enter with the handicap of an invitation which could be rejected if their conduct was unacceptable to the Supreme Communist in Moscow. In an entirely new government, all members would come in on the same basis.

Roosevelt was silent, except for the observation that the only problem was how to govern Poland. He inquired how soon there could be elections and suggested that the matter be referred to the foreign ministers. The Big Three had reached an impasse.

But Stalin could not resist heckling Churchill about the situation in Greece. "He had no intention of criticizing British policy there but he would merely like to know what was going on." Churchill reserved his explanation for the next meeting. Stalin deliberately chose Greece because British troops were seeking to prevent Greek Communists from seizing control. In the United States this action had been denounced as an example of British knavery.[12]

The evening was devoted to a banquet with Stalin as host. Cordiality was everywhere; forty-five toasts were drunk, most of them routine tributes. The three leaders sought to bridge their differences with compliments. Stalin proclaimed Churchill "the bravest governmental figure in the world." Because of Churchill's courage, England stood alone before Germany "when the rest of Europe was falling flat on its face before Hitler."

Churchill overlooked the time when Russia had been Hitler's eager ally. He praised Stalin "as the mighty leader of a mighty country, which had taken the full shock of the German war machine, had broken its back, and driven the tyrants from her soil."

Stalin lauded Roosevelt as "the chief forger of the instruments which had led to the mobilization of the world against Hitler."

[12] Plenary meeting, February 8, 1945, *ibid.*, 771–91.

93

Roosevelt described the banquet as a family dinner. Each of the leaders was working for the interests of their people. The objectives of the three leaders "were to give to every man, woman, and child on this earth the possibility of security and well being."[13]

Yet the good fellowship would only bridge momentarily the great political and philosophical gulf which separated Russia from her allies. Little weight should be given to these words spoken when the wine cups were full. The realities of international politics would prove more potent.

Sometime before the foreign ministers met on the morning of February 9, Roosevelt came to a decision over Poland. He dropped the idea of a Polish presidential committee and accepted the Soviet demand to reorganize the Lublin government by the addition of Polish leaders from London. He was afraid that unpleasantness on this issue might jeopardize the future United Nations. This "Polish Government of National Unity" would receive recognition by the three powers and hold elections in which "all democratic parties would have the right to participate and to put forward candidates." The Soviet, British, and American ambassadors in Warsaw would observe the elections and report on them to their governments.

When Stettinius proposed this at the foreign ministers meeting on February 9, Eden was unhappy because the formula appeared to favor the Lublin government. Molotov had to consult Stalin before making any decision.[14]

Although Stettinius contended that his formula would produce a new government, he was in error. The formula was essentially that of the Soviet Union and became the basis for the final decision of the conference. Roosevelt believed that the future United Nations needed Russia so badly that a formula should not stand in the way.

At the plenary meeting on February 9, Stettinius reported

---

[13] Dinner meeting, February 8, 1945, *ibid.*, 797–99.
[14] Foreign ministers meeting, February 9, 1945, *ibid.*, 802–14.

that the foreign ministers had agreed on the nations to receive reparations and the amount Germany would have to pay in kind. The United States and Russia had set the sum total for discussion by the future reparations commission at $20,000,000,000, with Russia to receive 50 per cent of the final figure.

On the Polish problem, Molotov proposed some changes in the wording which altered Roosevelt's draft slightly but stated more clearly that the Lublin government would be the foundation for the new Polish government. Molotov had suggested that there should be a reorganization of the Polish government with inclusion of "democratic leaders" from within Poland and from abroad. He objected to the United States plan for the ambassadors of the three governments to observe the elections and to ascertain if they were being carried out freely.

Roosevelt observed that they were very near agreement; it was only a matter of words. But more was at stake than words. He suggested that the foreign ministers meet that night and discuss the problem. Churchill was not as easily satisfied. He wanted the new government to be more broadly based than before the war when a minority had controlled Poland. For him there was a problem of lack of accurate information about Poland; in Britain there were rumors that the Lublin government would try members of the Polish Army as traitors. He would welcome the presence of the three ambassadors, and he reminded the meeting that as in Egypt whatever government conducted the election usually won.

Miffed at Churchill, Stalin retorted that in Egypt the politicians bought each other off; Egypt was not comparable to Poland where the people were literate. Stalin asked about the Egyptian literacy rate. Churchill lacked the information; he only desired a fair election. Roosevelt insisted that the election should be as pure as Caesar's wife. He added, "I did not know her but they said she was pure."

Stalin replied, "They said that about her, but in fact she had her sins."

In behalf of the Polish-Americans, Roosevelt asked Stalin for assurances that the elections would be "freely held." Stalin never answered the question but changed the subject. Roosevelt referred the problem to the overworked ministers.

After discussing the draft of a declaration on liberated Europe, the session ended.[15]

The next day, February 10, Eden and Churchill conferred with Stalin over the Polish question. Some agency, they argued, ought to report on events in Poland. Stalin declared that once the Polish government had been recognized, the British could send an ambassador who would be free to move about and report. He promised that the Red Army would not interfere. Without Roosevelt's support, Churchill and Eden could do no more except put their trust in Stalin's word.[16]

Roosevelt sought agreement on Poland, but not at the price of irritating Stalin. He conceded to Russian objections over the statement that the ambassadors should specifically observe and report on the elections. With this concession, the foreign ministers completed a formula for dealing with Poland at their meeting on February 10.[17]

When the plenary session opened in the afternoon, Eden reported for the foreign ministers. The Lubin government would be reorganized "on a broader democratic basis with the inclusion of democratic leaders from Poland itself and from Poles abroad." This provisional government would hold "free and unfettered elections as soon as possible on the basis of universal suffrage and secret ballot." The Russian, British, and United States governments would establish diplomatic relations with the provisional government, and their ambassadors would keep them informed about Polish affairs.

Roosevelt announced a change in his views regarding France. He accepted Churchill's view that the French govern-

[15] Plenary meeting, February 9, 1945, *ibid.*, 841–57.
[16] Churchill, *Triumph and Tragedy*, 385.
[17] Edward R. Stettinius, Jr., *Roosevelt and the Russians. The Yalta Conference* (ed. by Walter Johnson), 251–53.

ment could not administer a zone of occupation in Germany without membership in the control commission. Stalin reversed himself and concurred. Churchill had won a victory.

Reparations produced a heated argument. Churchill declared that his cabinet had instructed him to avoid any mention of a reparations figure; the matter should be left to the reparations commission. Roosevelt remarked that if any figure were mentioned, the American people would think of it in terms of money. Stalin bristled. He could not understand the confusion because the Soviet Union had treaties with Rumania, Finland, and Hungary in which the amount of reparations was stated. "If the British felt that the Russians should receive no reparations at all, it would be better to say so frankly," he declared.

For the first and only time during the conference, Stalin became excited. He rose from his chair gesturing to emphasize his argument. The conference ought to agree on the principle of German payment of reparations and authorize a reparations commission to sit in Moscow and determine the amount using an American-Soviet proposal for $20,000,000,000 with 50 per cent allotted to the Soviet Union.

Roosevelt demurred, claiming that the American people would think in terms of cash. Churchill proceeded to read a telegram from the cabinet insisting that no figure was possible until after an investigation. The figure of $20,000,000,000 was far beyond German capacity to pay. Stalin replied that the sum was only a basis for discussion.

Harry Hopkins, Roosevelt's special assistant, slipped the President a note suggesting that because the Russians had given in so much at the conference, the United States ought not to let them down. If the British desired to carry on the argument, they could do so in Moscow before the reparations commission.[18] Roosevelt then proposed that the matter be left up to the Reparations commission, but Eden and Churchill maintained that no sum should be mentioned. At Stalin's suggestion, Roosevelt and

[18] Hopkins to Roosevelt, February 10, 1945, *Yalta*, 920.

Churchill agreed to instruct the reparations commission to discuss the amount of reparations.

Then the Marshal requested a revision of the Montreux Convention because it was outmoded. Under the terms of this convention, the Turks could close the Straits of the Dardanelles at their discretion. Stalin complained that the convention had been drafted when Anglo-Russian relations had been poor, even the Japanese Emperor had a role in the affair. Stalin found it "impossible to accept a situation in which Turkey had a hand on Russia's throat." Perhaps the foreign ministers could consider revision of the convention.

Roosevelt observed that Canada and the United States had over three thousand miles of frontier without forts or armed forces. He hoped other countries would follow their example. Ignoring these comments, Churchill was sympathetic to Stalin and suggested that the foreign ministers consider the convention later in London. Stalin longed for an area that had been much coveted by the czars. For the present he had to curb his desires.

Roosevelt asked that changes be made in the statements regarding the Polish frontiers. Harry Hopkins had reminded him that some of the wording sounded as though Roosevelt was drawing frontiers, an activity which needed the approval of the Senate.[19] At Roosevelt's suggestion, the statement was altered to read:

> The three Heads of Government consider that the eastern frontier of Poland should follow the Curzon Line with digressions from it in some regions . . . . It is recognized that Poland must receive substantial accessions of territory in the North and West. They feel that the opinion of the new Polish Provisional Government on National Unity should be sought in due course on the extent of these accessions and that the final delimitation of the western frontier of Poland should thereafter await the Peace Conference.

[19] Hopkins to Roosevelt, February 10, 1945, quoted in Stettinius, *Roosevelt and the Russians*, 270.

Without Senate approval, however, Roosevelt had agreed to the eastern frontier of Poland. Just before the meeting ended, Roosevelt announced that he had to leave Yalta the next day at 3:00 P.M.[20]

The controversial decisions on the Far East were the result of private discussions between Roosevelt and Stalin. Since mid-December, Roosevelt had known about Stalin's major demands. On February 8, he had discussed the subject with Stalin; in the afternoon of February 10, he accepted Stalin's demands with slight changes. Churchill was not informed of the private agreement until the last day of the Yalta Conference. He signed the agreement over the loud objections of Anthony Eden, the British foreign secretary.

Stalin's chief demands called for a restoration of land and concessions taken from Russia by Japan as a result of the Russo-Japanese War. These included: the southern part of Sakhalin, the lease of Port Arthur as a Russian naval base, the internationalization of the port of Dairen, the Russo-Chinese operation of the Chinese-Eastern and South Manchurian railroads. Originally Stalin had demanded Russian control of Dairen and the railroads. The Japanese-owned Kuril Islands would be handed over to Russia. The *status quo* would be continued in Outer Mongolia, where the Mongolian People's Republic had become a Russian sphere of influence.

Stalin promised to enter the war against Japan "two or three months after Germany has surrendered." He would support the government of Chiang Kai-shek and seek Chiang's concurrence in the arrangements relating to Outer Mongolia and the railroads.

Roosevelt did not argue long over these demands except to obtain some modifications in favor of Nationalist China. He accepted these demands without lengthy bargaining lest Stalin refuse to help United States forces in the invasion of Japan. After American troops had conquered Japan with the loss of

[20] Plenary meeting, February 10, 1945, *Yalta*, 897–918.

many American lives, Stalin could order his troops into Manchuria and Northern China to seize whatever he desired. Certainly in February, 1945, Roosevelt and his associates considered the Kurils, Sakhalin, and concessions in Manchuria a small price to pay for Russian aid in the war against Japan when American invasion forces were expected to suffer very heavy casualties.[21]

In the evening at a dinner meeting where Churchill was the host, Stalin tried to convert him to the Russian view of the reparations question. How could he return and tell the Soviet people that he could not obtain reparations because the British were opposed? Churchill replied that he hoped Russia could receive reparations in large quantities, but after the last war they had placed the figure at more than German capacity to pay. Stalin asked for a statement in the final communiqué of the Allied intention to make Germany pay for damages inflicted on the Allied nations. Perhaps that night Churchill and Roosevelt were feeling mellow because the end of the conference was drawing near. They agreed to instruct the reparations commission to use the sum of $20,000,000,000 as a basis for discussion.

As the host for the evening, Churchill toasted his Russian guest. He declared:

> There was a time when the Marshal was not so kindly towards us, and I remember that I said a few rude things about him, but our common dangers and common loyalties have wiped all that out. The fire of war has burnt up the misunderstandings of the past. We feel we have a friend whom we can trust, and I hope that he will continue to feel the same about us.

There is no record of Stalin's reply.

When the conversation became general, Churchill mentioned the need for a general election after the defeat of Hitler. Stalin assured him that his position as leader was secure. There were two political parties in Britain, Churchill observed, and he belonged only to one. The Russian declared "One party is much better."

[21] Roosevelt-Stalin conversations, February 10, 1945, *ibid.*, 894–95.

When the conversation turned to the merry-go-round of French politics, Roosevelt commented that within one week he had dealt with three French premiers. During the past summer, De Gaulle had informed him of his intention to change this system.

As the evening drew to a close, Stalin remarked that he would never have signed the treaty with Hitler in 1939 except for the German-Polish Nonaggression Pact of 1934 and the Munich Agreement. Churchill and Roosevelt kept silent.[22]

When Stalin left the dinner, Churchill led the British delegation in cheers for the Soviet premier. Yet neither cheers nor toasts could bridge the fundamental political differences between the two democracies and the Soviet Union. When peace came again, these differences would remain to plague the world.

The last meeting, on February 11, was devoted to polishing up the protocols and communiqués. At 3:34 P.M. the conference adjourned. Roosevelt would never again meet with Churchill or Stalin.

The Yalta Conference has been damned as a surrender of vital American interests through secret deals. In the frustrations brought on by the Cold War, Churchill and Roosevelt were accused of giving Stalin control of Central Europe and turning Chiang Kai-shek out of China. In retrospect these accusations are false.

Yalta did not determine the political control of Europe. Military realities drew the map, beginning with the decision at Teheran that an Anglo-American invasion would come through Western Europe and that Russian armies would enter Europe from the east. After the terrible German attack, Russian troops could only be removed from Central Europe by force. With these troops Stalin could fasten his hold on the new Russian empire.

Many of the fundamental conflicts were postponed at Roo-

[22] Dinner meeting, February 10, 1945, *ibid.*, 921–25; Churchill, *Triumph and Tragedy*, 390–93.

sevelt's insistence lest they impair Allied unity. Perhaps Church-ill and Roosevelt should have argued out their differences with Stalin over the future of Europe. But with a world war yet to be won, they dared not take the risk. Clauses and words would have to paper over the disagreements.

Roosevelt and Churchill made their greatest concession on paper in regard to the Polish government. Apparently they be-lieved they had approved the formation of an entirely new coali-tion government. Actually they accepted the reorganization of the Communist (Lublin) government in Poland by the "inclu-sion of democratic leaders from Poland itself and from Poles abroad." In Moscow these words were interpreted to imply that the Communist (Lublin) government would be the base and other leaders would be added. Because Russian troops would occupy Poland, Stalin and his associates would decide which "democratic" (i.e., friendly to Russia) leaders would be ad-mitted to the Polish government.

Roosevelt and Churchill probably obtained the best pos-sible compromise from Stalin regarding Polish elections. Once the new, enlarged Polish Provisional Government of National Unity had been formed, "free and unfettered elections [would be held] as soon as possible on the basis of universal suffrage and secret ballot." More than this Stalin refused and Roosevelt would not demand. Guarantees to insure honest elections were lacking. The only guarantee of honest elections in the western style would have been international supervision which Stalin would never permit within his new empire.

At Yalta, Roosevelt, Churchill, and Stalin had to grapple with an impending massive change in the balance of power. Talk and paper agreements served to hide the change. Russian armies were thrusting far into Central Europe. In the Pacific, Stalin expected that his demands would be granted in return for Russian aid. Despite Russian casualties, destruction, and suffer-ing, he craved compensation befitting Russia's new power posi-tion. In the future Russian co-operation would be required to help keep the peace. For the present Russian troops were needed to win the war. To Churchill and most of all to Roosevelt, the Yalta Conference was neither the place nor the time to have a showdown over the postwar balance of power.

Roosevelt went to Yalta with little preparation for the conference, but he was confident that he could manage Stalin. To a friend he remarked before the Conference: "Stalin? I can handle that old buzzard."[23]

Through his handling, he hoped to bring Stalin into full co-operation with the West in the postwar world. For that reason he let Churchill be the advocate of the Poles. For the same reason he was prone to pass unpleasant problems on to the foreign ministers without firmly coming to grips with them.

Roosevelt has been credited with being the arbiter of the Yalta Conference, but whatever arbitration he exerted was minimal and passive lest Stalin be aroused. The effect may have been to lead Stalin to believe that in any future showdown with Churchill over Central Europe, Roosevelt would be neutral.

Roosevelt was handicapped by his country's history of isolation. He thought in terms of Midwestern senators and congressmen angrily demanding the return of "our boys." This explains his announcement, so alarming to Churchill and so delightful to Stalin, that American troops would have to be pulled out of Europe two years after the end of the war. Churchill feared that the British and the French would be left alone facing Stalin whose troops would be thrust far into Central Europe. The Prime Minister fought to preserve the big-power status of Great Britain and to bring the French to his support. Too often it seemed that Roosevelt was deserting him.

Stalin had done his homework well. He stubbornly insisted on his demands, yet he did not get all that he wanted. In Germany his greatest goal was denied him. He secured Poland, but only because his troops were in control. Britain and the United States could not start another war before finishing the old one.

[23] Gunther, *Roosevelt in Retrospect*, 356–60.

They needed Stalin to help them, particularly in the Far East.

The plunder he obtained was not a surprise to the others. Much of the loot had at one time been either Russian or Russian-held, and the Japanese had taken most of it in the Russo-Japanese War. Should Russia be denied her rights because of Japan? If the Russians wanted to take the Kuril Islands, who would deny them Japanese territory? Roosevelt did not dare face American mothers and tell them that their sons had to die because he would not allow Stalin the Kuril Islands in order to get his help.

In accepting Stalin's bill for the Far East, Roosevelt gave up nothing that the Russian armies could not have taken easily without an agreement. Without booty, Stalin might have stayed out of the war in Asia. In 1939, Stalin allied with Hitler who offered more loot than could Britain and France. The Japanese would have been pleased to make a deal to keep Russia out of the war.

In 1945, General Douglas MacArthur, commander of the United States forces in the Far East, and Admiral Ernest J. King, commander-in-chief of the United States fleet, both welcomed Russian participation in the war in Asia. When American troops stormed ashore on the Japanese beaches, if Russian help had saved American lives and shortened the war, concessions granted Stalin in the Far East would have been applauded. Later the agreement seemed unnecessary because the atomic bomb forced Japan to surrender. Should Roosevelt then be condemned because he was not a prophet?

The secrecy surrounding the Far Eastern Agreement made it appear sinister and exaggerated its importance. Secrecy seemed necessary in order to avoid a heated public debate in the United States where Chinese affairs were cloaked in righteousness and sentimentality. Publicity would have aided the Japanese and impelled them to make Stalin a counter offer. Could he have resisted temptation if Tokyo offered more than he had obtained at Yalta?

The Far Eastern Agreement only reinforced the decision

made at Cairo in 1943: Japan would lose her empire and influence in Asia.

At the Yalta Conference, Roosevelt was intent on obtaining British and Russian co-operation in establishing the United Nations organization. He wanted no repetition of the sad history of the League of Nations when great powers had often been absent. For Roosevelt, the decision to call the conference of the United Nations before the war ended was a mighty victory. Unencumbered by territorial questions and treatment of the defeated, the delegates could concentrate on drafting the charter for the new world organization. They would avoid Wilson's error of mixing negotiations over a peace treaty with the drafting of the Covenant of the League of Nations.

Disenchantment over Yalta developed after the wartime Allies had quarreled over postwar Europe. Then the men of Yalta were blamed for all of the troubles that had plagued the world since 1945. Ambitious politicians wrenched the agreement out of its historical context and held it up to scorn. They forgot it had been signed while a war raged and when men of good will needed the help of Russian armies.

Yalta has been used to prove the dangers of the summit conference. This is unfair because it was no worse than other conferences which suffered from the same ills. The realities of power left no way for the terms of the Yalta Agreement to be enforced short of war. If the Yalta Agreement had been carried out according to Western interpretations, history would have been different. The Yalta Conference would have been praised instead of cursed.

· 8 ·

Between War and Peace

I<small>N THE SPRING</small> of 1945 as Allied armies closed in on the remnants of Hitler's once mighty armies, thorny problems bedeviled the politicians. The Soviet government evaded the spirit and letter of the Yalta Agreement. Under threat of Soviet guns and tanks, a Communist government took office in Rumania on March 2.

The Polish situation failed to improve. In Moscow, Clark Kerr and Harriman battled with Molotov over the formation of a broader Polish government. Molotov insisted on his own interpretation of the Yalta Agreement. To Churchill this was a test case of Russian sincerity. To stop Molotov's tactics, Churchill proposed to Roosevelt a direct message to Stalin on the issue. The President was loath to resort to personal intervention until all else had failed. At last on March 29, Roosevelt agreed to complain to Stalin over Poland.

Stalin's reply was uncompromising. The American and British ambassadors had snarled up the Polish problem by insisting on a new government instead of reconstructing the Lublin government. The Poles invited from London would be in the minority, and they must be fully desirous of friendly relations between Russia and Poland. If his desires were not met, Stalin declared, the Polish problems would be settled in a short time. Stalin inferred that he would ignore his allies.[1] To show his displeasure, he threatened to keep Molotov from attending the San Francisco Conference on the organization of the United Nations.

He accused his allies of betraying Russia through negotiations with German forces in Italy and promising a soft peace. In anticipation of the end of the war in Italy, he alleged, German troops were being transferred to the Russian front.

The death of President Roosevelt on April 12, 1945, produced a major change in United States leadership. The new President, Harry S. Truman, was totally inexperienced in foreign affairs, coalition warfare, and dealings with Russia. He had to feel his way in administration and somehow find that grasp of foreign policy which comes only with time and experience, but time he could not have. Truman wanted to follow Roosevelt's policies toward the Soviet Union, hoping that Russian distrust and suspicion would somehow lessen; he wanted to implement the Yalta declaration although some of his advisers insisted that the United States had no responsibilities in Central Europe.

Churchill was fearful of Soviet policy, particularly in Poland where he desired to fulfill the Yalta Agreement. Stalin rejected Churchill's ideas of a new Polish government because he wanted the Communist provisional government to become the legal government of Poland, basing his attitude on the need for a friendly government.

[1] Churchill, *Triumph and Tragedy*, 743–45, 437–39.

British and American attempts to study conditions in Poland, in accord with the Yalta agreements, were rebuffed. Future policies for Germany and Austria were uncertain; in the former German satellites, Communists seized control with slight pretense of legality.

In Vienna, the Russians formed a provisional government and refused to allow the American and British missions to enter and to observe. As Hitler's armies collapsed, Anglo-American armies pushed into Germany and even into Czechoslovakia. Churchill implored Truman to agree that they use these gains for bargaining over the future of Poland, the organization of Germany, and the conditions in the nations now occupied by Russian armies. Truman would not agree, preferring to withdraw American troops to occupation lines that had already been agreed on with the Russians.[2]

Events so disturbed Churchill that on May 6, 1945, he wrote Truman about the need for a meeting of the three heads of government while the Anglo-American forces still held their positions in Europe. Although Truman was agreeable to a summit conference, he wanted the suggestion to originate with Stalin. He suggested that Churchill "induce Stalin to suggest or request such a meeting."[3] The President would not come until sometime after June 30 because of the need to prepare the budget.

Churchill then proposed a meeting somewhere in Germany outside the Russian occupation zone for early July. "Twice running we have come to meet him," he complained. Churchill begged Truman to confer with him before any meeting with Stalin. He doubted that Stalin would propose the meeting, but he would accept an invitation.[4] Like Roosevelt, Truman refused

[2] *Ibid.*, 511–16.

[3] Truman to Churchill, May 9, 1945, *Foreign Relations of the United States, Diplomatic Papers, The Conference of Berlin (The Potsdam Conference)* (hereafter cited as *Potsdam*), I, 4.

[4] Churchill to Truman, May 11, 1945, *ibid.*, 5.

a meeting with Churchill prior to a meeting with Stalin lest it seem they were "ganging up" on the Soviet leader.[5]

The views of Truman and Churchill were at variance. Distressed and fearful of the future, the Prime Minister was troubled by the withdrawal of American troops from Europe, the reduction in British forces, the French weaknesses and perversities, and the Russian enigma. "An iron curtain is drawn down upon their front. We do not know what is going on behind," Churchill warned the new President. He considered it vital to reach an understanding with the Russians before the armies were weakened, but this could only be accomplished through a personal meeting. "This issue of a settlement with Russia before our strength has gone seems to me to dwarf all others."[6] Truman would not cancel the instructions for American armies to withdraw to their occupation zones, nor would he rush into a conference because other pressing affairs required attention. Some of his associates warned him to beware of the Churchill wiles, for the Prime Minister sought to use naïve Americans to further the interests of the British Empire. They believed that Britain sought to build Western Europe into a British sphere of influence, composed of France, the Netherlands, Belgium, Denmark, and Norway; it would be "something in the nature of dominion status in the British Commonwealth." Such a bloc would alarm the Russians and strengthen the British opposition to the Russians. The joint chiefs of staff believed that the future threat of war could come only from Anglo-Russian quarrels. "So long as Britain and Russia co-operate and collaborate in the interests of peace, there can be no great war in the foreseeable future." Any formation of power blocs or British spheres of influence would only arouse Russian suspicions.[7]

Such influences led Truman to dispatch Joseph W. Davies to confer with Churchill and explain the American attitude. Davies was a presidential adviser, a millionaire, and a former

[5] Truman to Churchill, May 11, 1945, *ibid.*, 8.
[6] Churchill to Truman, May 12, 1945, *ibid.*, 8–9.
[7] Briefing Book Paper, "British Plan for a Western European Bloc," *ibid.*, 256–66.

ambassador to Russia, who believed wholeheartedly in the cause of Soviet Russia and accepted official Russian statements at face value. The Davies mission seemed imperative to some of Truman's associates because they feared the Prime Minister might become so distraught over Russia that he would destroy the wartime unity.[8]

Davies spent eight hours talking with Churchill, explaining Truman's policies, querying him, and lecturing him on his attitude towards Russia. As Davies explained Truman's views, a meeting of the three heads of government was imperative to compose the growing differences over Yalta and to solve the problems developing from the victory in Europe. Truman believed that a crisis threatened only because of the Soviet suspicion that Britain and the United States were "ganging up" on their ally. Davies declared that, before the trio conferred, Truman wanted to meet alone with Stalin.

When Churchill reviewed the world problems, according to Davies' written report, the Prime Minister became "vehement and even violent in his criticism of the Soviet armies and officials." He feared the "steel curtain" that was being clamped on Eastern Europe, and dreaded withdrawal of the American army. Davies rebuked Churchill for such language and lectured the Prime Minister on the "legacies" of suspicions which hurt Allied unity. Churchill's attitude so shocked Davies that he wondered if "the Prime Minister, was now willing to declare to the world that he and Britain had made a mistake in not supporting Hitler, for as I understood him, he was now expressing the doctrine which Hitler and Goebbels had been proclaiming and reiterating for the past four years in an effort to break up allied unity and 'divide and conquer.'" Davies avowed that the Soviet leaders could be relied on to work for peace and co-operation in Western Europe.[9]

Truman sent Harry Hopkins to Moscow to talk with Stalin

[8] William D. Leahy, *I Was There*, 369–70.
[9] Davies to Truman, June 12, 1945, *Potsdam*, I, 64–78.

and to invite him to the conference. Through Hopkins, Truman hoped to reassure Stalin of the sincerity of United States policies. Between May 26 and June 6, Hopkins had six meetings with Stalin which revealed wide differences. Stalin insisted that "it is therefore in Russia's vital interests that Poland should be both strong and friendly."[10] He placed all the blame on the British for the Polish troubles, and he announced his intentions to weaken or destroy the London Poles.

Hopkins informed Stalin that Truman was ready to meet in the Berlin area about July 15. The date was satisfactory with Stalin but not with Churchill, who pleaded for an earlier meeting because of the increasing problems. Truman rejected Churchill's pleas and the Prime Minister had to accede to the President's wishes.

Preparatory to the meeting, the participants were briefed by their staffs on the issues to be faced. Only the briefing papers of the United States delegation are available for study, and these reveal a thorough study of the problems and possible solutions. Despite the Soviet actions in Europe since the Yalta meeting, the Americans believed that by hard negotiating they could achieve their goals. They were optimistic in contrast with Churchill's pessimisms and fears which were ignored or slighted; his worries were diagnosed as the result of the general election and fears over the decline of British power.

The United States delegation traveled by ship and used the sea voyage for rest and study. Truman was as well prepared as he could have been in view of his inexperience and personality. He came to the conference out of necessity; he did not welcome such a meeting as had Roosevelt. For Truman it was an onerous chore. "Wish I didn't have to go, but I do and it can't be stopped now," he wrote his wife and daughter as he prepared to leave. On board ship, he was still unhappy: "I wish this trip was over. I hate it. But it has to be done."[11]

10 Sherwood, *Roosevelt and Hopkins*, 900.
11 Harry S. Truman, *Year of Decisions*, 331, 338.

Fearful of the future and with Davies' complaints fresh in his mind Churchill went to Potsdam expecting little help from Truman. Anticipating trouble from Stalin during the conference in the form of a *fait accompli* in Central Europe, he was not the self-confident leader of the days of Dunkirk and the Battle of Britain but a worried prophet.

About Stalin's frame of mind, the historian can only speculate. In the conference he was calm and unhurried, speaking quietly to his interpreter, Pavlov. He could be relaxed because his regime had not only been saved, but his empire had been enlarged and much of Central Europe was now occupied by his troops. Stalin knew the Anglo-Americans could not forcefully challenge him because they needed his aid in the assault on Japan. Even if he had foreseen that the atomic bomb would shorten the war and reduce the need for Russian aid, he would not have altered his tactics. Stalin did not have to concede anything because he had received the necessary help from the West, and his realm was secure. The capitalist states seemed to need his aid in settling European problems and returning to the ways of peace. Western climate of opinion opposed a fresh war against Russia over the control of Central Europe, particularly Poland.

Stalin's domination of Poland had increased without serious Anglo-American opposition. In March, sixteen important members of the Polish government in London were invited by the Soviet military authorities to Warsaw for discussions over co-ordinating the Polish resistance movement with the final Soviet campaign against Germany. The sixteen were taken to Moscow, arrested, and charged with activities harmful to the security of the Russian army. They were tried, and twelve were sentenced to long prison terms. Thus Stalin eliminated potential leaders of any Polish opposition to his rule.

While the sixteen were on trial, a conference opened in Moscow over the formation of a new Polish government in accordance with the Yalta Agreement. Harriman, Molotov, and Archibald Clark Kerr, the British ambassador, consulted with

Poles from Warsaw and London. The new government which the conference produced was dominated by Polish Communists who would do Stalin's bidding. July 5 the United States and Britain recognized the new government of Poland.

The opening of the conference was delayed because of a slight heart attack suffered by Stalin. In the interval, Churchill visited Truman on July 16. Their talk was without political significance lest they seem to be teaming up against Stalin. The pair were far apart in views and personality, but the meeting seemed pleasant for both. Truman learned that he could meet Churchill without sacrificing United States interests for the British Empire.

Truman was impressed by Stalin when he called on the President at the Little White House on July 17. Truman "talked to him straight from the shoulder," he reported to his wife. "I felt hopeful that we could reach an agreement that would be satisfactory to the world and to ourselves." The President promised to "deal directly with Stalin as a friend and that, since he was no diplomat, he would not beat around the bush but would operate on a 'yes' or 'no' basis." Stalin announced that the Soviet Union would enter the war against Japan by mid-August after completing negotiations with the Chinese government over the Manchurian railroads and the status of Darien and Port Arthur.[12]

Truman did not use this opportunity to press for Russian moderation in the demands that were being made on China. Ambassador Averell Harriman had cabled the State Department concerning Russian demands for a majority of the directorships on the railroad and a Soviet military zone which included Port Arthur and Darien. Because of his desire to insure that Russia entered the war against Japan, Truman may have been reluctant to press the Chinese question. Perhaps it did not seem too important when compared with the host of other problems awaiting solution by the heads of government at the summit conference which was about to convene.

[12] *Ibid.,* 341–42; Bohlen memorandum, March 28, 1960, *Potsdam,* II, 1584.

9

Potsdam, 1945

A T 5:00 P.M. on July 17, 1945, the three leaders and their teams of advisers assembled in the reception room of the Cecilienhof Palace, a former residence of the last Hohenzollern crown prince. They seated themselves around a large circular table, the flags of the three nations in the center, and each leader flanked by his advisers—fifteen men to deal with the problems of war-torn Europe at the summit of power.

Stalin proposed that Truman preside over the meetings and Churchill concurred. Using this opportunity, Truman presented an agenda headed by a proposal for a council of the foreign ministers of Russia, Great Britain, France, the United States, and China to begin consideration of the various peace treaties. The President submitted a memorandum on the treatment of

Germany, and then he read a declaration calling for the implementation of the Yalta Declaration in liberated Europe, particularly Rumania and Bulgaria. Truman wanted steps taken to alter the status of Italy because he felt that the time had come to admit Italy into the United Nations. Churchill suggested that the Polish problem be added to this list. Stalin added reparations, the division of the Germany navy and merchant fleet, territories to be placed under trusteeship, and relations with the former colonies of the defeated states. When Churchill called for "careful consideration" of Truman's proposals, he inferred that Truman's haste was ill-advised; they ought to take their time. The Prime Minister suggested that the foreign ministers furnish the heads of government with an agenda from this collection.

Truman and Churchill were agreeable to Stalin's suggestion that for the present they discuss the formation of a council of foreign ministers. They succeeded only in agreeing that China should not be a member of the group because neither Stalin nor Churchill was eager to have China involved in the affairs of Western Europe.

As the meeting broke up, Truman observed: "There should be some issue to discuss on which we can come to a conclusion tomorrow." Churchill thought that the foreign secretaries could find some points to keep them busy.

"I don't want just to discuss, I want to decide," Truman insisted.

"You want something in the bag each day," joked Churchill.

The busy president retorted, "I should like to meet at 4:00 instead of 5:00."

"I will obey your orders," replied Churchill.

Stalin could not miss the opportunity and inquired, "If you are in such an obedient mood today, Mr. Prime Minister, I should like to know whether you will share with us the German fleet."

"We will share it with you or sink it," joked Churchill.[1]

[1] Plenary meeting, July 17, 1945, *Potsdam*, II, 52–63.

At the plenary meeting of July 18, Truman's proposal for a council of foreign ministers to draw up peace treaties with the satellites and prepare for the peace conference with Germany was accepted in principle. China was eliminated from European questions because the European peace treaties would be prepared by those who had signed the treaties of surrender. The Truman plan for political control of defeated Germany was accepted. Russion objections were slight because Germany would be governed by the Control Council on which Stalin's generals would sit and oppose whatever displeased him. German military power would be destroyed; war criminals would be tried; and German economy would come under Allied control.

A Soviet plan that all assets, armaments, and troops of the London Poles be turned over to the new Polish government produced a lengthy speech from Churchill, who reviewed the problems and heartaches in setting up the Polish forces. A just and fair solution must be reached on the future of these men, he declared. The British policy was to persuade as many as possible to return to Poland, but he feared that many might not go back, thus inconveniencing Britain. Churchill praised the valor of the Polish troops who had fought beside their British allies in Germany and Italy. He was determined to treat them honorably, and if they did not wish to return to Poland, they must be taken into the British Empire. Stalin objected because the London Poles were still in action although official recognition had been withdrawn. They must be quieted. Churchill politely refused to silence them.

Stalin replied that he understood Churchill's difficulties and did not want to worsen them; he only sought to end the Polish government-in-exile and would withdraw any item that bothered Churchill. Truman saw no fundamental difference in their points of view, but he had more interest in free elections in Poland. At Stalin's suggestion the matter was referred to the foreign ministers.[2]

[2] Plenary meeting, July 18, 1945, *ibid.*, 88–98.

The third plenary meeting on July 19 opened with a discussion over the disposal of the German navy and merchant fleet. Stalin, eager to have his share, insisted on division into thirds with other powers excluded. The principle was accepted with the stipulation that the German merchant fleet would be used in the campaign against Japan.

A bitter argument developed between Stalin and Churchill over policy towards Spain. Stalin wanted the conference to recommend that the United Nations break off all relations with Franco, support the "democratic forces in Spain," and aid the Spanish people in creating a government responsive to their will. He contended that foreign intervention had produced the regime, not the Spanish people. Churchill insisted that to break off diplomatic relations with Spain would only rally around Franco many segments of the population which might have deserted him. To break off relations with a nation because of "its internal conduct of affairs was a dangerous principle." Truman "had no love for Franco," but he wanted the Spanish people to decide the question. Stalin argued that Franco was gaining strength, and it was not an internal affair. The Spanish people ought to know that the three governments had taken a stand against Franco. Realizing that he could not change their opinions, Stalin proposed that the foreign ministers study the matter. Churchill refused because this was a matter of principle, and as long as he participated in the British government there would be no interference in internal affairs of a nation. Stalin was willing to insist only on an "appraisal" of the Franco regime, but Churchill rejected that as well as Stalin's next proposal to have an appraisal of all countries. At Truman's suggestion they left the question.

Turning to Yugoslavia, Churchill desired that the Yalta Declaration on freedom be carried out there because the Yugoslav leaders, Tito and Ivan Subâsič, had so promised. These men had signed agreements in 1944 calling for the formation of a Yugoslav government representing all political views and which would hold free elections and guarantee civil rights. Instead, Tito had created a controlled press and a one-party government and repressed civil rights. The British government had given him much material support during the war, and now he had disappointed his friends.

Stalin was suddenly very considerate of Yugoslav feelings although he had given Tito little aid against the Germans. He knew nothing about Churchill's allegations that disagreement existed among the Yugoslavs over Communist rule. He had no knowledge of any infringement of Yugoslav civil rights. With Churchill, he was agreeable to calling Yugoslav leaders to present their case.

Truman interrupted the argument. He had come as the representative of the United States but not as a judge to settle affairs that should eventually be heard by the United Nations. "I want to discuss matters on which the three heads of government can come to agreement," he declared. "I did not come to hear Tito, de Gaulle, and Franco."

"That is the correct observation," Stalin commented.

Churchill observed that the United States was interested in fulfilling the Yalta Agreement; President Roosevelt had attached great importance to carrying out the declaration, and that was all he wanted. Truman admitted that complaints over Yalta had been received; he wanted the declaration carried out. Stalin retorted that Tito was complying with the declaration, Churchill's information notwithstanding. At Truman's insistence, the matter was postponed.

The three heads of government gave their final approval to the establishment of the Council of Foreign Ministers, whose chief task was to draft peace treaties and propose territorial settlements. France, Britain, Russia, China, and the United States would send their foreign ministers. Those states which had signed the surrender terms would share in the peace making.

This would prevent the Chinese from becoming involved in European problems.[3]

Truman brought up his proposal for a preliminary agreement with Italy in the plenary meeting of July 20. Until the peace treaty would be negotiated, the Italians would refrain from hostile action and maintain only those armed forces permitted by the Allies. Allied control would continue as long as required by the military situation and until the territorial problems were solved. Stalin immediately suggested that it be referred to the foreign ministers. At the same time, he wanted consideration of similar treaties for Finland, Hungary, Rumania, and Bulgaria.

Churchill was critical of Truman's proposals. He could not forget Italian attacks on Britain while she stood alone; other nations that had suffered losses fighting Italy—New Zealand and Australia for example—ought to be consulted. Churchill questioned if the present Italian government was really a democratic government and could honestly carry out the United States' proposals. Yet he was more sympathetic to this treaty than to those with the other satellites.

Stalin was more inclined towards Truman's proposal than the Prime Minister, hoping to use it for his own purposes. He had no objection to the proposal in principle because, despite Italian sins, they must do everything to get her on the side of the United Nations and separate her from Germany. The same principles applied to the other former German satellites who had caused much suffering to the Soviet Union. Stalin only asked that diplomatic relations be resumed with the satellites, whose governments were no more democratic than that of Italy.

Truman interrupted to insist that they get back to the subject: Italy. However, he was willing to reach agreement on the matter of the satellites. He wandered off on a discourse about the huge sums of money which the United States was pouring into Europe without getting anything in return; the United States

[3] Plenary meeting, July 19, 1945, *ibid.,* 116–37.

could not continue indefinitely supporting these governments. At this conference they must create favorable conditions to enable these countries once more to help themselves. He wanted the matter referred to the foreign ministers for agreement on all these countries; his colleagues concurred.

The meeting ended with a wrangle between Churchill and Stalin over Austria. Churchill complained that the British officers could not enter Vienna to inquire about accommodations nor could their troops enter the occupation area of Austria that had been assigned to them. The United States and British troops had withdrawn to their occupation areas in Germany, but the British were not allowed into Austria.

Stalin retorted that the agreement on Austrian control had only been completed. Truman explained that he had signed the necessary documents that same day. Stalin turned on Churchill. Why was Churchill so indignant? Although Soviet officials were not permitted in the British sector of Germany, they did not complain because they understood the problems in moving troops. Stalin had no objection to the armies occupying their zones in Austria and Vienna.[4]

On July 21 the foreign ministers produced the results of their efforts to resolve the Polish problem. The most important disagreement concerned free elections and the reporting of these elections by the press. The British had sought a strong statement pledging the Polish government to conduct their elections in such a manner that the world would know that "all democratic and anti-Nazi sections of Polish opinion have been able to express their views freely." Strong objections to such unpleasant inferences came from the Russians. Anthony Eden agreed to soften the statement if there was an assurance that the press would have full freedom to report on Polish activities before, during, and after the elections.

Stalin was sensitive for the Poles who were "very touchy

[4] Plenary meeting, July 20, 1945, *ibid.*, 164–82.

and will be hurt." They might suspect the three heads of government "of accusing them of being unwilling to accord a free press." He wanted the press requirement eliminated. Truman reminded Stalin that the United States was concerned with Polish elections. He had six million Polish voters to consider, and they would be easier to handle if a free press could report on Polish elections. Stalin agreed, and a statement on the freedom of the press was included although it was not strong enough for Churchill. Stalin could appear magnanimous over freedom of the press because his troops occupied the nation, and any complaints over election irregularities could be treated as the work of antidemocratic elements.

The foreign ministers could not decide whether the Italian treaty should be taken up simultaneously with the treaties for the other Nazi satellites. Truman insisted that the questions be treated separately because the United States had been unable to recognize the other satellites. He accepted Stalin's suggestion to pass over the matter. Churchill complained that "time was passing, that the Heads of States had been here for a week and that many papers had been passed over," but he agreed with Truman's position.

At last they came to the question of the Polish frontiers. Truman objected because the Poles had occupied German territory as far west as the Oder and Neisse rivers without consulting the other powers. Stalin claimed that the Germans had fled leaving only Poles who had to set up some administration. Where was the harm? The Soviet Union was not bound in this matter by the Yalta Conference. He wanted the rear areas quiet; the restoration of German administration in this area would be too difficult.

Churchill complained that the British and the Americans had to feed large numbers of Germans who had fled the disputed territories. But Stalin would not have the Poles feeding the Germans, cultivating their fields, and giving them food. Churchill argued that the 1937 area of Germany should be available to all of Germany irrespective of the zone in which the food was produced.

According to Stalin, either the Poles ran their area or the economy would collapse because there were no Germans in the area. The Germans were to blame for their troubles. "Our policy is to create difficulty for the Germans in order to make it difficult for German power to rise again," he said. Why should the United States and Britain object to creating obstacles for their business rival? The less German industry there is, the better market for United States and British goods. There was nothing more that could shake Stalin although Churchill reminded him again of starving people in the British and American zones. Stalin retorted, "There will be none." Truman admitted that they were at an impasse. The meeting adjourned.[5]

They were still at an impasse when Poland was discussed on July 22. The Polish Communist government wanted the Neisse-Oder line as the western frontier because this would give them control of the area which they were then occupying. Truman wanted to pass it over and consider it later. Churchill reiterated his arguments over the frontier. Stalin retorted that there were enough fuel resources for all the Germans in the Ruhr and Rhineland, if Churchill was worried because of the loss of Silesian coal fields. He contended that all of the Germans were gone from the area.

Knowing how the Polish Communist leaders would view the subject, Stalin proposed that they be invited to confer with the Council of Foreign Ministers, which would be operating by September. Truman was willing because no agreement then seemed possible, but Churchill was reluctant to wait so long and consented to Stalin's next proposal that they be brought to the Potsdam Conference. Truman could not see the need for speed, but Churchill realized that the longer the Poles stayed in German territory, the more they would become masters of the

[5] Plenary meeting, July 21, 1945, *ibid.*, 203–21.

area. He wanted a provisional frontier with the Poles recognized as Russian agents, but Truman was opposed. Stalin put it up to them: either do it themselves without the Poles or invite them. All agreed to an invitation.

It was time to steal some colonies. Molotov put forth the Russian request for discussion of the trusteeship procedures, particularly who would have the Italian colonies in the Mediterranean. The trick did not escape Churchill, who reminded them of British expense in lives and ships while fighting the Italians. Britain had not made any claims in the Baltic as the Russians had done for Königsberg. Let any who claimed them put forward their demands at the peace conference. He said that he could not see what the Russians wanted, but he well knew what they wanted. He was cool, curt, and definite: no Russian colonies in the Mediterranean.

The last important topic for that day's discussion was the revision of the Montreux Convention which governed the Straits of the Dardanelles. On an earlier visit to Moscow, Churchill had indicated to Stalin that he was sympathetic on this matter. Now he warned Stalin that Turkey must not be unduly alarmed by the revision. Molotov explained that the Turks had asked about an alliance, but the Soviet Union wanted changes in the frontiers and the abrogation of the Montreux Convention. Turkey and the Soviet Union would ensure freedom of navigation and protect the straits; to that end Soviet bases would be established in the straits. This was another Russian theft, but discussion was postponed for the moment while the British and Americans studied the documents presented by Molotov.[6]

In the meeting of July 23, the Russian demand for a base in the Straits of the Dardanelles came up again. Churchill would not support the Russian claim nor did he think that the Turks would do so. Stalin reminded him that the day before he had alleged that the Turks were frightened because of the large numbers of Russian troops in Bulgaria. Stalin declared that

[6] Plenary meeting, July 22, 1945, *ibid.*, 244–68.

Churchill's information was incorrect; he insisted there were fewer Russian troops in Bulgaria than British troops in Greece, where there were five British divisions. Two, Churchill retorted. The Marshal asked about the number of British troops, and Churchill declared that there were only 40,000. The Russians, Stalin then announced, had 30,000. Churchill held his tongue, but British intelligence sources estimated 200,000 Russian troops in Bulgaria instead of 30,000.

Stalin launched into a long complaint over the situation of the straits where Turkey could decide when to close them against Russia. "The result was that a small state supported by Great Britain held a great state by the throat and gave it no outlet." A Russian naval base was necessary to protect the straits because Turkey was too weak; the base must either be in the straits or near enough to defend the entrance to the Black Sea. Stalin compared his demand with the situation of the United States in Panama and the British in Suez.

Truman interrupted with a reference to all wars within the last two hundred years starting in an area between the Black Sea, the Baltic, and French and Russian frontiers. The conference must prevent a repetition, and they could help by arranging for passage of goods and vessels through the Straits on an unrestricted basis. Truman then advocated unrestricted navigation on inland waterways bordering on two or more states and regulated by an international authority. He proposed that they begin with the Danube and Rhine, and he would have the United States, the United Kingdom, Soviet Russia, and France as members of the International authority. He did not want another war twenty-five years later over the Danube or the Straits. Churchill had to agree, and stated his preference for an international guarantee of the Straits instead of a Russian base. Stalin had to study Truman's proposal.

Next on the day's agenda was the Soviet demand for the transference of the port of Königsberg, an old Prussian city on the Baltic, to Soviet Russia. Although both Churchill and Truman expressed sympathy, neither would agree forthwith. Stalin accepted Churchill's suggestion to put it off until the peace conference.

The next item was a Russian demand for a conference over France and Syria, then under British occupation. Churchill insisted that British troops were there only for the French and would be happy to withdraw whenever they could. He was cool towards a conference after the British had borne the entire burden; however, he would be happy if the United States wished to replace the British. Truman declined the invitation. When he saw that Churchill would not be embarrassed, Stalin withdrew his proposal. Churchill then requested the withdrawal of Soviet troops from Iran. Stalin refused until six months after the defeat of Germany and her allies. The matter was referred to the foreign ministers.[7]

In the evening of July 23. Churchill hosted a banquet with Truman sitting on his right and Stalin on his left. Stalin proposed the next meeting in Tokyo. Throughout the evening the banqueteers moved about changing seats. Churchill succeeded in having a friendly talk with Stalin who commented enthusiastically about Russian entrance into the war against Japan. He seemed to expect a long war. During the evening, Stalin went about the table and collected autographs on his menu.

In the usual toasts, Churchill praised Truman's "sincerity, frankness, and power of decision." Truman explained that because "he was naturally a timid man," he had been overwhelmed when Churchill and Stalin proposed that he preside over the conference. It had been "both a pleasure and privilege for a country boy from Missouri to be associated with two such great figures as the Prime Minister and Marshal Stalin." Stalin praised Truman's modesty as a "source of strength and a real indication of character."[8] The next day they returned to their quarrels.

On July 24 most of the meeting was spent squabbling over

[7] Plenary meeting, July 23, 1945, *ibid.*, 299–319.
[8] Churchill, *Triumph and Tragedy*, 668–69; *Potsdam*, II, 319–21.

Italy and the other German satellite states. The United States and Britain were agreed on a peace treaty with Italy, drawn up by the Council of Foreign Ministers. Then the Italian application for membership in the United Nations could be considered. Peace treaties with Rumania, Bulgaria, Hungary, and Finland could next be prepared, and after these treaties had been concluded with "responsible democratic governments," applications for the United Nations would be supported.

Stalin objected to the creation of an abnormal situation for Bulgaria, Rumania, Hungary, and Finland by treating them as lepers. It was an attempt to discredit the Soviet Union. He saw little merit in the case of the Italians because although they had surrendered first, yet they had done more damage than the other German satellites. Italy had not held any democratic elections, and neither had the others. Truman interjected that Italy was different from the rest because Britain and the United States had free access. He wanted democratic reorganization along democratic lines as laid down in the Yalta Agreement. Stalin retorted that the governments of Finland, Hungary, Rumania, and Bulgaria were more democratic than Italy's because they were not Fascist. "If a government is not Fascist, a government is democratic," he announced.

Churchill insisted that there was a difference because Italy had been out of the war for two years, and the British representatives had been in the country, lived there, and knew the conditions. There was no censorship; the Prime Minister was attacked daily in the newspapers. They knew nothing about Bulgaria and Rumania; the British mission in Bucharest was practically interned. Stalin retorted, "All fairy tales!" Churchill had confidence in his representatives. The difference was that in Italy, the Russians were welcomed and could go anywhere. Stalin, however, retorted that it was otherwise: "The Russians had no rights in Italy."

Molotov proposed that each of the three governments consider "separately in the immediate future," the establishment of diplomatic relations with Finland, Bulgaria, and Hungary. Truman was silent, but Churchill rose to battle. The establishment of diplomatic relations would mean recognizing Communist satellite regimes. Stalin, supported by Truman, questioned the legality of signing peace treaties with unrecognized governments. Finally the trio compromised on preparing treaties "*for*, not with these countries."

When they returned to the Straits question, Truman insisted that his proposal about the inland waterways be considered along with Stalin's demands. When Churchill, with Truman's support, advocated a guarantee of the Straits by the three governments, Stalin and Molotov counterattacked with criticism of British control over the Suez. When Stalin saw that Truman and Churchill were not going to let him have his booty, he was willing to postpone the Straits question.

As the leaders and the members of their delegations were chatting quietly after the meeting, Truman sauntered over to Stalin and casually informed him about the successful explosion of the first atomic device on July 16 at Alamogordo, New Mexico. Stalin seemed pleased and hoped it would be put to good use against the Japanese. Probably his lack of surprise resulted from knowledge of American atomic research that had been supplied him by Soviet agents. In the subsequent discussions there was no indication that the news of the explosion in any way influenced either his tactics or attitudes. Nor did the possession of this new force alter the plans and arguments of Truman and Churchill, who chose not to exploit their advantage. It is doubtful that American public opinion then would have supported any attempt by Truman to use the new force as a threat to extract concessions from Stalin. Truman and Churchill neither used this opportunity to discuss peaceful use of atomic energy nor offered to share their knowledge with the Soviet Union.[9]

The July 25 meeting was consumed by a Stalin-Churchill wrangle over Poland and the refugee question. Churchill com-

[9] Plenary meeting, July 24, 1945, *ibid.*, 357–74.

plained about Poles in the Russian zone driving Germans out of their occupation area without considering the food supply. Stalin saw nothing wrong with taking revenge on the Germans.

Truman opposed the Polish policy, but he would not decide the German-Polish frontiers then but left them to be determined at the peace conference. Next he lectured Stalin and Churchill on the United States Constitution. Although he might support a proposal in the conference, it would still have to be considered in treaty form by the Senate. He concluded with the pious wish that "world peace could only be maintained by the three of them present at the table."

His hearers understood his constitutional dilemma but fell to wrangling again. Stalin argued that coal and iron from the Ruhr were more important than food; Churchill required that these be paid for with food from the Russian-Polish zone to feed the Germans in the British zone. Stalin replied that as Germany had always imported food, there would not be enough for the western zone. Even the Poles, he revealed, had asked Russia for food. Churchill reminded the Marshal that Britain faced a coal-less winter because of the shortage; it was even necessary to export coal to Holland, France, and Belgium. Stalin saw no reason why the British did not make the Germans dig coal for them; there were forty thousand German soldiers in Norway who could become coal miners. The Russian situation was worse than Britain's because Russia had lost over five million men. Stalin feared that if he complained, "Churchill would burst into tears so difficult was the situation in Russia."[10]

This proved to be the last argument between Churchill and Stalin. The Prime Minister returned to Britain the next day to learn the results of the British general election. When they were announced, Clement Attlee, who had been a silent participant in the meetings, was the new prime minister. When the heads of government assembled on July 28, Atlee and Ernest Bevin, the

[10] Plenary meeting, July 25, 1945, *ibid.*, 381–91.

foreign secretary, represented Great Britain. Soon the three heads of government were entangled in an argument over the invitations to join the United Nations and recognition of the former German allies; they could only agree to postpone the argument.

The argument was almost as confused on Italian reparations. Truman announced that the United States and the British government had contributed $500,000,000 to the feeding and rehabilitation of Italy. His government did not propose to give Italy money in order for Italy to pay reparations. Stalin complained that the Soviet people would not understand because Italy had sent troops to the Volga River. He tried to draw out some sum that the Italians could pay, but Truman did not know how great the amount might be. Attlee and Bevin hastened to support Truman. They had no objection to military equipment; Stalin was willing to have that, and he asked only for agreement in principle. Truman seemed sympathetic to his demands, provided that the Anglo-American claims were considered first. Attlee did not commit himself although Stalin tried to force agreement out of him by reminding him of what Italy had done to Britain. They adjourned without any firm decision.[11]

Because of Stalin's cold the heads of government did not meet until July 31. In the interval, the United States delegation had produced a package deal on Poland and reparations. The Russians had demanded $500,000,000 of shares in industrial and transportation concerns in the Western zones, 30 per cent of German foreign investments, 30 per cent of the German gold in Western hands. Instead, Secretary of State James F. Byrnes proposed that 15 per cent of the unnecessary industrial capital equipment in the Western zone of Germany would become reparations, and the Russians would trade foodstuffs and minerals for this amount. They would receive an additional 10 per cent without giving anything in exchange. After a heated argument,

[11] Plenary meeting, July 28, 1945, *ibid.*, 459–70.

Stalin agreed to drop his earlier demands. This was a partial victory for the Western delegations because there was no specific sum demanded by the Russians.

Regarding the Polish frontier, a proposal of the United States was accepted which turned over a zone of Germany to Polish administration pending the final determination of the frontier by a formal peace conference. The area lay east of a line from the Baltic, then to Swinemünde, along the Oder River to the Western Neisse River and down to the Czechoslovak frontier. Although they did not realize it then, the Western statesmen had determined the Polish frontiers.

Stalin brought up a proposal for international control of the Ruhr which would be separated from Germany. An Allied council with United States, Russian, British, and French representatives would administer the Ruhr for the purpose of extracting reparations. Truman and Bevin rejected Stalin's suggestion; the Ruhr was a part of Germany and would be administered by the Control Council.

They agreed on the economic principles for the government of Germany with little difficulty because the reparations question had been settled. In quick succession less important matters were decided: transfer of German minorities, German fleet, and merchant marine.[12] On August 1 two meetings were held in which final changes were made in the agreements of the conference. The summit meeting ended at 12:00 A.M., August 2.

Knowing that Churchill's position was the weakest, Stalin deliberately baited him during the conference while Truman watched the contest. Never did Stalin harass Truman as he did Churchill. Perhaps Stalin hoped that Truman, like Roosevelt, might be inclined to be anti-British.

At the Potsdam Conference more use was made of the foreign ministers than in the previous wartime summit conferences. Before the plenary meetings they met to seek solutions to prob-

[12] Plenary meeting, July 31, 1945, *ibid.*, 510–38.

lems referred to them; unresolved issues they presented to the three heads of government. Molotov conceded only on points that did not endanger the Russian position. Eden tried to uphold his nation's interests as well as secure the Yalta Declaration; he worked well with his American colleague James Byrnes, the newly appointed secretary of state. For the South Carolina aristocrat and former Supreme Court justice, the Potsdam Conference was the beginning of an education in the ways of the Soviet Union and its leaders.

On paper the work of the summit meeting was impressive. Unlike 1919, plans had been made to settle the final peace problems and to clear up the wreckage of war; the control of Germany had been settled and the reparations question apparently solved. Given wholehearted Soviet co-operation, the Potsdam Agreement might have produced an orderly Europe. However, Russian determination to establish a new empire in Eastern Europe ruined whatever might have come from Potsdam. The Soviets did not satisfy their desires over reparations, but they did make the West accept a *fait accompli* in Poland.

The American delegation came away from Potsdam with the belief that it had been a successful conference because arrangements had been made for the Council of Foreign Ministers to prepare for the peace conference and thus avoid the mistakes made in Paris in 1919. Their joy was short lived because the peace conference was delayed until 1946 when treaties were at last signed for Italy, Rumania, Bulgaria, Hungary, and Finland. The Austrian treaty did not come until 1955, and at the present time there is still no treaty for Germany. The Potsdam Conference never accomplished the United States' aim to make such satisfactory arrangements for the ending of the war in Europe that American troops could be fully withdrawn and military expenditures reduced.

It is doubtful that the presence of Churchill throughout the conference would have altered the results. Nor would the presence of Roosevelt have changed the outcome fundamentally; the pressure to concede might have brought a split with Churchill or Attlee.

The Potsdam Conference failed because of American naïveté over the establishment of democratic governments in Central Europe and because of the inability and reluctance of the Anglo-American forces to exert power. Stalin contributed to the failure by his grab for loot and his refusal to permit the full implementation of the Yalta Declaration lest anti-Communists win honest elections. If the British and American leaders had been in a position to exert military power, Stalin might have acted differently.

Potsdam became one more chapter in the education of the West in the tactics and goals of Soviet diplomacy, which were old-fashioned, bourgeois, power politics. Stalin's ruthless snatching for territory to enlarge the Russian empire would have gladdened the hearts of Peter I, Catherine II, and Alexander I. Now it only increased the suspicion and fears of the West, fostering a spirit of unity before the Soviet threat.

The presence of the heads of government did not speed up decision-making. Nor were the decisions any more significant by virtue of their presence. A great deal was postponed, and nothing decided which fundamentally altered the power position on the continent of Europe, once the armies had withdrawn to their lines of occupation.

The Potsdam Conference has been condemned for surrendering territory, but this denunciation is an injustice to Western leaders when Stalin's attempted expansion is considered. He cynically sought as much strategic territory as possible; the list of loot which he tried to steal is frightening. The demand for $10,000,000,000 in reparations would have kept all Germany under some form of Russian control for an indefinite period. A separate Ruhr under international control would have given Russia a voice in the government of an important industrial area and prevented economic recovery of Western Europe, particularly West Germany. Stalin tried to obtain release from the Yalta pledges for "the earliest possible establishment through free elections of governments responsive to the will of the people." He sought outright recognition of the puppet governments which had appeared in the wake of the Russian armies in eastern Europe. He presented the conference with a *fait accompli* in the Polish-German boundary, and by handing German territory over to Polish control he sought to make Poland more dependent on Russia. Reverting to the old czarist dream to control the Straits of the Dardanelles and Constantinople, Stalin boldly demanded an end to the Montreux Convention and claimed the right of Russia to establish a military base near the Straits of the Dardanelles. Such a base would have threatened the independence of Turkey and ultimately have converted her into another Russian satellite. Attacks on British policy in Greece were launched in an effort to force them out because their presence hampered Stalin's plans for domination. He tried to involve Russia in the administration of the Italian colonies, particularly Libya with its strategic position on the North African coast. To further his domination of Iran, Stalin requested that the Soviet Union be excused from the obligations to withdraw the occupation troops from Iran until six months after the end of the war. He tried to force discussions of the British role in Syria and Lebanon with the hope that Russia might enter these nations as collaborators in an international administration. To promote Russian interests in the western Mediterranean, Stalin tried to have the international control of Tangier altered.

Stalin put these demands shrewdly and expertly without any Marxist verbiage, in the best tradition of his czarist predecessors. Perhaps he thought that the conditions were so favorable that an attempt was worthwhile. The United States was uninterested in the fate of these territories, seeking only to get her troops home and demobilized. The British would be left alone, weakened after the war, and unable to resist without United States' help. The need for Russian help in the war against

Japan ought to make the British, and particularly the Americans, ready to grant Russia concessions in order to have her help. They could not deny him anything that he already controlled without a fresh war while that with Japan was not yet over; whatever could be acquired would be worth the effort.

If Stalin had been victorious in his campaign, the results for the free world would have been disastrous. All of Germany would have been under the threat of Russian blackmail; Greece and Turkey would have gone the way of Bulgaria and Rumania; the Mediterranean would have been under increasing Russian control; and Iran would have become another Russian satellite. It is to the credit of Western statesmen that Stalin did not depart with more. Where Soviet forces could only be ejected by fighting, there Stalin seized and secured his victory: Poland, Bulgaria, Hungary, Rumania, and Eastern Europe. Without the presence of Russian troops, his efforts failed.

10

A Cold War Summit?

For a decade after the Potsdam Conference, the Cold War dominated East-West relations and wrecked any possibility of a high-level meeting. Western leaders learned that "democratic" governments mentioned in the Yalta and Potsdam agreements must be wholeheartedly pro-Russian in order to survive in Soviet-dominated Europe. The former wartime allies quarreled over German reparations. Negotiations over a German peace treaty collapsed in 1947. The Truman Doctrine and the Marshall Plan heralded a more active United States policy in Europe. In 1948, Czechoslovakia became an unwilling Soviet satellite. The same year, Russian forces failed to drive the Western troops out of Berlin with the blockade. Through the Berlin blockade, Stalin hoped either to control Berlin completely or to obtain a voice in governing the western zones of Germany. He used the ensuing breakdown in the four-power control of Germany to fasten his grasp on East Berlin and East Germany. As a shield against further Soviet aggression, the western European nations and the United States formed NATO (North Atlantic Treaty Organization) in 1949. The outbreak of the Korean War in 1950 only heated up the Cold War. The United States looked to its defenses at home and abroad. Plans were soon under way to give West Germany a role in the defense of Western Europe. Under these conditions a summit conference over East-West issues was impossible.

By 1953 significant events required policy changes. In Washington the newly installed Eisenhower administration pledged important measures for peace. Stalin died in March leaving a government that might be more inclined to negotiate with the West. The Korean War came to an end without a peace treaty.

In Great Britain, Winston Churchill had returned to office as prime minister. Even while in opposition he had called for "another talk with Soviet Russia upon the highest level." He advocated "a supreme effort to bridge the gulf between the two worlds so that each can live their life, if not in friendship, at least without hatreds of war."[1]

On April 20, 1953, he voiced his interest in a meeting of the principal powers in the Cold War. Churchill hoped that nothing would impede the working of good will until there would come "conversations on the highest level even if informal and private, between some of the principal powers concerned." The House of Commons showed its approval by its applause.[2]

Speaking in the House of Commons on May 11, 1953, Winston Churchill called for another summit conference, declaring that it was a mistake to "assume that nothing can be settled with

[1] *Parliamentary Debates, House of Commons,* Fifth Series, Vol. 473, Cols. 199–200.
[2] *New York Times,* April 21, 1953.

Soviet Russia unless or until everything is settled." He proposed that "a conference on the highest level should take place between the leading powers without long delay." He rejected a conference confined by a rigid agenda, lost in details, and surrounded by officials. "The conference should be confined to the smallest numbers of powers and persons possible." Churchill wanted the conference to meet "with a measure of informality and a still greater measure of privacy and seclusion." Even if they did not achieve all their goals, the Prime Minister argued that at least intimate contacts would be established between the leaders. If they were completely successful, the result would be "a generation of peace."[3]

Both British political parties welcomed the suggestion although it encountered some opposition from the Foreign Office. Paris was alarmed lest Churchill's call for a small number of powers meant the exclusion of France. The most important reaction had to come from the United States. There the new Republican administration was hostile to such a meeting, particularly after Republican speakers had belabored the Democrats over Yalta in the presidential campaign.

The State Department rejected discussion until the Russians showed good faith. Senator William A. Knowland, Republican majority leader, damned Churchill for urging a "Far Eastern Munich." President Dwight D. Eisenhower informed a cabinet meeting: "This idea of the President of the United States going personally abroad to negotiate—it's just damn stupid. Every time a President has gone abroad to get into the details of these things, he's lost his shirt."[4]

Moscow was silent until American reaction to Churchill's speech had been fully reported. Then the Soviet government announced its interest in Churchill's proposal but rejected all preconditions required by Washington.

[3] *Parliamentary Debates, House of Commons,* Fifth Series, Vol. 515, Cols. 883–98.

[4] Emmet John Hughes, *The Ordeal of Power,* 151.

Any meeting of the heads of government in 1953 would have been impossible because of the Washington political climate. There the junior senator from Wisconsin, Joseph McCarthy, through bluff, lies, and double talk had chained the already timid American foreign policy. His lust for power made him the most dreaded figure in Washington. Neither Eisenhower nor Dulles dared fight him in 1953. McCarthy opposed a summit conference.

Churchill continued to advocate a summit meeting until Secretary of State John Foster Dulles agreed to an Anglo-French-American conference at Bermuda in June, 1953. When Churchill suffered a stroke, the meeting was cancelled. Once his health had been restored, Churchill again sounded the call for a summit meeting in a speech at the London Guild Hall on November 9. In a meeting with Eisenhower and Dulles at Bermuda in April, 1954, Churchill appealed without success for a summit conference. Two months later in Washington, he again failed to convince Eisenhower and Dulles of the need for a summit conference.

Speaking in New York at the United Nations on November 22, 1954, French Premier Pierre Mendès-France proposed a four-power conference in Paris, organized by his government if the other three nations approved. The next day Eisenhower replied that there could be no meeting at the summit until after the ratification of the Paris agreements and adequate preparation for the conference through a meeting of the foreign ministers.

Ratification of the Paris agreements seemed assured in March, 1955. By these agreements West Germany would receive full independence and enter the North Atlantic Treaty Organization.

The Soviet government, realizing that its battle against the Paris agreements had failed, proposed a four-power treaty ending Austrian occupation. The Russian concessions were so extensive that agreement was soon reached. To many, Russian withdrawal from an eastern European nation foretold a new era in Soviet policy.

In Washington on March 20, 1955, Senator Walter F. George, chairman of the powerful Senate Foreign Relations Committee, advocated a four-power meeting that same year.[5] Such strong support from the opposition party was decisive in changing United States policy. The State Department, voicing Dulles' views, declared that the Senator's proposal was in line with department thinking. The change in American policy was influenced by the Austrian negotiations, the belief that Russia was experiencing such domestic troubles that a relaxation of tension would seem appealing, and a fear that Communist China might start a war over Matsu and Quemoy.

To his news conference on March 23, Eisenhower declared that he was ready to go anywhere for peace. Although there might be propaganda at such a conference, the world must hope that at a new conference some constructive step could be taken to start the world on the path toward "a better agreement."[6] On March 25, Premier Edgar Faure of France announced that he held similar views.

Prime Minister Anthony Eden, who had succeeded Winston Churchill, thought the moment was right to prepare for discussions with Russia because the position of the West relative to that of Russia would not improve with the passing of time.[7] Moreover, an impending general election on May 26 quickened Eden's interest in a summit conference because the Labor opposition favored such a meeting.

On May 10, in a tripartite note to the Soviet government, the three Western powers declared that the time had come for a fresh attempt to resolve the problems confronting them. They invited the Soviet government to join "in an effort to remove the sources of conflict between us." They suggested meetings of the heads of the four governments and their foreign ministers to formulate issues for consideration and to decide on methods for

[5] *New York Times*, March 21, 1955.
[6] *Ibid.*, March 24, 1955.
[7] Anthony Eden, *Full Circle*, 320.

exploring solutions. The second stage would be to work out the problems using the basic principles laid down by the heads of government.[8]

Unconsciously they had echoed the sentiments of Neville Chamberlain who had also desired in 1938 to remove sources of discord through a policy known as "appeasement," so recently damned by the Republican party in political speeches. By refraining from a detailed agreement on the problems and by seeking issues that needed solution, Western leaders hoped to avoid another Yalta Agreement.

When the four foreign ministers met in Vienna on May 15 for the signature of the Austrian State Treaty, Molotov, still Soviet foreign minister, informed them that his superiors would gladly come to such a conference. In official reply on May 26, the Soviet government criticized the United States for approaching the conference from a "position of strength." United States leaders had even announced their intention to interfere in internal affairs of the peoples' democracies. The Soviet government rejected such a deplorable policy. The United States had proposed an international meeting to consider international problems but at the same time announced plans to deliberately ruin the conference. Nevertheless, the Soviet government accepted the invitation and agreed to begin the summit conference in Geneva on July 18.[9]

When the United Nations General Assembly met in San Francisco, June 20, the four foreign ministers discussed details of the summit meeting. Molotov, on his best behavior, raised few objections to the Western proposals. The conference would last four to six days; the chairmanship would rotate, beginning first with Eisenhower; there would be no formal agenda, rather the heads of government would discuss anything they thought disturbed the peace. In an opening statement each leader would

[8] *The Geneva Conference of Heads of Government, July 18–23, 1955* (hereafter cited as *Geneva*), 6–7.
[9] Soviet note, May 26, 1955, *ibid.*, 7–9.

outline what he considered to be the main causes of tension and the best procedures to be followed to reduce them. The heads of government would meet in the afternoon and the foreign ministers the following morning to take up the ways and means of handling questions raised by the afternoon sessions. Molotov was cool towards the time limit and Western reluctance to negotiate specific problems.[10]

By the spring of 1955, Dulles and Eisenhower were free of the shackles imposed on them by McCarthy and his cohorts. Even the members of the Senate found enough courage to defeat a McCarthy resolution 77–4 on June 22. McCarthy had demanded prior agreement to discussion on Eastern Europe and Communist Asia before any conference convened.

Dulles had long opposed any summit conference, but his attitude had changed. He favored negotiating from strength, and now he believed that Russia was weakening while Western forces were gaining in strength. Russia, he thought, was on the verge of an economic collapse. His change in attitude may have been speeded by the Democratic majority in Congress which favored a summit conference.

Russian rulers, however, had differing views on Soviet strength. Nikita Khrushchev, the first secretary of the Communist Party, and Nikolai Bulganin, now the Russian premier, appeared at the July 4 celebration at Spasso House, the American Embassy in Moscow. Khrushchev served notice on the West that the Soviet Union was still vigorous. If the Western powers did not want to talk seriously at Geneva, the Soviet Union could "wait and hold on." If they talked honestly and sincerely, "something will come of it." He complained that some wanted "to wait until our legs are broken" before reaching an agreement. The Soviet Union, he warned, would ignore Western reluctance to negotiate definite agreements.[11]

In the evening of July 15 as Eisenhower's plane was pre-

[10] *New York Times,* June 21, 1955.
[11] *Ibid.,* July 5, 1955.

pared for departure to Geneva, the President went on television and radio. In this conference, he informed a nationwide audience that he hoped to "change the spirit that has characterized the intergovernmental relationships of the world during the past ten years." The postwar conferences had dealt with too many detailed, specific problems and had failed to establish the spirit and attitude in which to approach them. Successes were few, and the conferences were used to exploit "nationalistic ambitions" and to broadcast propaganda. One ingredient had been missing: "An honest intent to conciliate, to understand, to be tolerant, to try to see the other fellow's viewpoint as well as we see our own." If a new spirit could be infused in a conference, a major step toward peace could be taken. He ended with a request for universal prayer "to demonstrate American sincerity and feeling for peace."[12] Privately he confessed: "Personally I do not expect any spectacular results from the forthcoming 'Big Four' conference."[13]

Dulles did not expect to reach a truly sincere agreement with the Russians. He agreed to the conference because public opinion required a high-level effort. Perhaps the West might see through Soviet tactics. Dulles knew that a major agreement with the Soviet government would be possible only if the West was prepared to accept the *status quo* in Germany and eastern Europe. He was not so inclined.

Within the Western camp all was disunity. There was no unified plan for the conference. Eden did not like the rigid timetable; there was too much rushing. He asked for preliminary meetings of the Western heads of government but Eisenhower refused. Eden believed that they were not allowing themselves enough room for maneuver. By assigning topics to each head of government, they were staging a play. Faure was concerned about security and disarmament; Eden wanted to press for Ger-

[12] *Geneva,* 13–16.
[13] Dwight D. Eisenhower, *The White House Years. Mandate for Change 1953–56,* 506.

man unification. Eisenhower had another idea. He proposed "to define the crucial world problems and then issue a directive to the foreign ministers to work out the details and conduct negotiations."[14]

But already the correspondents had begun to arrive on the shores of Lake Geneva. Over twelve hundred representatives of the press came to cover the summit conference. Lobbyists and agents of the German Federal Republic thronged the city where evangelist Billy Graham ended a five-month preaching mission with the announcement: "Never before have so many looked to so few for so much. The next six days may be the most important in the history of the world."[15]

[14] Eden, *Full Circle*, 323, 328; Eisenhower, *Mandate for Change*, 508.
[15] *New York Times*, July 18, 1955.

11

Geneva, 1955

THE FIRST plenary meeting of the four heads of government opened in the afternoon of July 18 in the Palais des Nations, where the old League of Nations had labored over world problems. Instead of the private, man-to-man talks suggested by Churchill, more than forty men sat down at four large tables arranged in a square. Additional assistants and observers sat in rows behind the heads of governments and their associates.[1] A boxing ring in the center would have completed the picture of a private fight club. The four governments had brought over twelve hundred people to this conference.

[1] *Illustrated London News*, July 23, 1955, pp. 136–37. A photograph in a two-page spread shows ninety-three men and women in the room during a plenary session.

As the only chief of state present, Eisenhower acted as chairman and opened the conference. He hoped they could "create a new spirit that will make possible future solutions of problems." The President proposed German unification with an all-German government based on free elections. Ten years had passed since the end of the war, he observed, but Germany was still divided and still a source of instability. Eisenhower was prepared to take into account the legitimate security interests of the Soviet Union. The peoples of Eastern Europe had never received the full benefits promised them by the wartime declarations of the United Nations. Problems of communication and contact between the East and West should be discussed as well as international Communism which created distrust and sought to subvert lawful governments. Eisenhower proposed a study of disarmament; they should seek dependable ways to supervise and inspect military establishments. He concluded: "Let me repeat, I trust that we are not here merely to catalogue our differences. We are not here to repeat the same dreary exercises that have characterized most of our negotiations of the past ten years."[2]

Faure advocated an end to the Cold War by solving the German problem through electing an all-German government and drafting a peace treaty. The Premier wanted Germany within NATO, but to quiet Russian fears, he stressed its defensive nature. Disarmament must come within some kind of international organization. An international economic-organization could utilize the funds derived from disarmament for helping the underdeveloped countries. If a nation lowered its contribution to the fund or ceased altogether, then the world would know that rearmament had begun.[3]

Eden emphasized the need to unify Germany because this divided Europe. All four ought to join a security pact which included Germany. Each would promise to assist the victim of aggression. They should reach agreement on the forces and arm-

[2] *Geneva*, 18–22. [3] *Ibid.*, 22–31.

aments which each side should maintain in Germany. A control system would be needed to supervise this arrangement. The conference ought to consider a demilitarized zone between East and West.[4]

Bulganin announced that the conference would play a great role if everyone showed "a genuine desire to achieve relaxation of international tension and bring about a feeling of confidence between nations." The arms race must end and atomic weapons must be banned. He wanted the conference to reach agreement on the size of their armed forces; he was prepared with suggested figures. A system of collective security involving all Europe and the United States should be created; then NATO, the Paris Agreements, and the Warsaw Treaty must end. This system should aim at ridding Europe of foreign troops. Although he supported German unification, Bulganin was cool towards remilitarization and membership in NATO. As for the peoples' democracies in Eastern Europe, he saw neither need nor authorization for discussion of this question. It was "common knowledge that the regime of people's democracies has been established in those countries by the people themselves of their own free will." Bulganin closed with a request for the strengthening of economic ties and the broadening of international contacts in culture and science.[5] The Premier's remarks indicated a line from which there would be little variation in the next few days.

After the first day's talks, the foreign ministers drew up an agenda including reunification of Germany, European security, disarmament, and development of contacts East and West. Molotov insisted on adding the termination of the Cold War, encouragement to neutrality in Europe, and the Far Eastern problems.

Eisenhower gave a dinner for the Russians that evening. Nothing of importance was said by the Russian quartet: Bulganin, Khrushchev, Marshal G. K. Zhukov, Soviet defense minister, and Andrei Gromyko, Soviet foreign minister. They ap-

[4] *Ibid.*, 31–34.   [5] *Ibid.*, 35–43.

peared more interested in watching each other. Eisenhower and Zhukov had been friends during the war, but when the President took the Marshal aside, he muttered: "There are things in Russia which are not as they seem."[6]

In the plenary meeting of July 19, Eisenhower accepted Bulganin's demand to drop discussion of the east European satellites and international Communism. The President refused to discuss the Taiwan question without Nationalist China being represented.

Bulganin argued that Germany must be free of any military obligations to the West. Unification was not the chief problem. "Germany," Bulganin declared, "is not united now and therefore some time must elapse before it is united." Any hopes that the others had of laying the groundwork for German unification were now ended.

The Soviet Premier scorned Eden's proposal for a five-power security pact. Such an arrangement might suffice for a small, weak power, but it was unsatisfactory for a strong power like Russia which could not depend on the guarantees of others. If West Germany remained in NATO, the union with East Germany would not soon be achieved. Bulganin proposed that both Germanies draw closer together through a security pact and through trade. Once confidence had been created, and a general security system had ended opposing blocs, then Germany might be united.

Bulganin had revealed the Russian price for German unification: a Germany without any ties to the West and particularly to NATO. Unless the West conceded, the status of Germany would not change.

Eisenhower appealed to his old comrade in arms Marshal Zhukov. "I have known him for a long time and he knows that, speaking as soldier to soldier, I have never uttered a single word that I did not believe to be the truth."

"We believe you," Bulganin interrupted.

[6] Eisenhower, *Mandate for Change*, 517–18.

The President insisted that Germany must not be allowed to become a military vacuum and thus become a fertile ground for another Hitler. He reminded the others that all of the world knew the activities of the Western nations. The United States, for example, could declare war only after free debate and a vote of Congress.

NATO was purely defensive, the President argued. Germany would be limited within NATO because no member of the alliance would make an aggressive move. Germany would have her forces entwined with the other members of NATO. There would be no need to fear a united Germany within NATO.[7]

Faure protested the delay in reunification. Eden was angered by the Soviet rejection of his security proposals. His limited pact would be quicker to negotiate, but the Soviet plans would take years to negotiate. Eden could not see why his proposed pact "wounded" the Soviet delegation.

That evening at a dinner given by Eden for the Russians, Bulganin and Khrushchev discussed their problems with him. Bulganin reiterated the Russian fear of German recovery. Eden understood their fears because Britain had no reason to feel tenderly towards Germany after two world wars, but they must look to the future. Bulganin declared that it would be impossible to return to Moscow if the Russian delegation agreed to immediate German unification. "This was something that Russia would not accept . . . neither the army nor the people would understand and this was not the time to weaken the government." The people would claim that Stalin would never have agreed to this.[8]

Eisenhower had desired to avoid specific proposals, but on July 20, Bulganin and Khrushchev presented a general treaty of collective security including all of the European states, both Germanies, and the United States. An attack against one would be an attack against them all. None of the parties to the

---

[7] *Time* (August 1, 1955), 17; Eden, *Full Circle*, 331; *Geneva*, 45–46.
[8] Eden, *Full Circle*, 333–34.

Circumstances at the Potsdam Conference in 1945 forced President Truman to allow Stalin to keep his hold on Eastern Europe. The conferees at this meeting were (from left to right) Winston Churchill, Harry S Truman, and Joseph Stalin.

Courtesy Wide World Photos

The Geneva Summit Conference of 1955 was no less disappointing than former meetings. French Premier Faure, third from left, appears puzzled as fellow conferees laugh during picture-taking session at the Palace of Nations. From left to right are Nikolai Bulganin, Dwight D. Eisenhower, Edgar Faure, and Sir Anthony Eden.

treaty could conclude any agreement contrary to the purposes of this treaty. Pending final arrangements on the reduction of armaments, the parties would promise not to increase their troops in Europe.[9]

NATO would have been ended by such a pact because the parties to the treaty could not join in any agreement contrary to the treaty. United States troops stationed in Europe would have been limited but not Russian troops within the Soviet Union.

Eisenhower complained that the Russian delegation seemed to believe that an over-all pact, deferring German unification would contribute more to security. To develop such a plan would only confirm the division of Germany which the West thought contributed more to insecurity. They could not bring about unification merely by saying that they believed in eventual unification. The President charged that they were now taking up matters of detail which could not be handled in the absence of other interested nations. They ought to turn this matter over to the foreign ministers with the request that they devise some kind of machinery or plan another conference.

Eisenhower had admitted that the heads of government could not agree on what they were supposed to do. He hoped that somehow the foreign ministers would deliver the heads of government from their dilemma. His suggestion was accepted, but the foreign ministers found agreement just as difficult.

As if released by flood gates, proposals flowed into the conference on July 21. The Russians produced a new variation of their old attempt to break NATO with a nonaggression pact between NATO and the Warsaw Pact nations until a collective security arrangement had been completed. The Warsaw Pact placed troops of the Soviet bloc under Russian command and permitted the stationing of Russian troops within the satellite nations.

Next Bulganin and Khrushchev brought up a disarmament

[9] *Geneva*, 48-52.

treaty requiring a reduction in size of the armed forces and a solemn promise by the atomic powers not to use such weapons while negotiations proceeded towards complete prohibition. There would be an immediate pledge to discontinue testing these weapons. At an undisclosed time, international control would establish methods of reducing armaments and prohibiting atomic weapons.

The Russian disarmament plan gave Eisenhower the opportunity to introduce his "open-skies" proposal. This had grown out of discussions of a panel of experts set up under Nelson Rockefeller to study recommendations that the United States might submit to the Geneva Conference. From their studies of reports on European opinion, the panel hit upon the idea of aerial inspection and exchange of military information as the means of calming European opinion alarmed over atomic weapons and the presence of American troops in Europe. The idea had been considered at a meeting of Eisenhower's advisers on July 19 in Geneva. At the end of a two-hour meeting, they agreed that Eisenhower ought to present the proposal, with Harold Stassen to draft a general statement on disarmament and Eisenhower to write out detailed notes for his presentations. Bulganin's disarmament proposal gave the needed opening.

On July 21, Eisenhower gave priority in disarmament study to inspection and reporting. To this end and to show the sincerity of the United States government, he proposed for them to arrange an exchange of "a complete blueprint of our military establishments, from beginning to end, from one end of our countries to the other; lay out the establishments and provide the blueprints to each other." Each would provide the facilities for aerial photography for the other to take and then to study.

As Eisenhower finished presenting his plan, a loud clap of thunder shook the room as it was plunged into darkness. From the darkness, Eisenhower observed that he had never imagined that he was "so eloquent as to put the lights out."

Bulganin immediately declared that the proposal "seemed

to have real merit." However, the Soviet delegation would have to study it. The conference recessed for the day. As Eisenhower came up to Khrushchev afterwards, the Soviet leader declared: "I don't agree with the chairman." At this remark, Eisenhower finally realized who the real power was in the Soviet delegation. His labors to convert Khrushchev to his plan were without success because the Soviet leader considered that "the idea was nothing more than a bald espionage plot against the U.S.S.R."[10]

The open-skies proposal contradicted the essentials that Eisenhower had laid down as the foundation for the conference: avoidance of detailed agreements. He meant it as a basis for consideration, but it would not be considered seriously by representatives of a nation whose government had always been bent on keeping out foreigners.

What was to be included in the "blueprint?" Munitions factories? What type of installations? Would the Russians include their space program which was then well under way? Might not these revelations profit one side more than the other? Had such an exchange any support among congressional leaders? How did Eisenhower and Dulles ever seriously consider such a proposal except as a part of the propaganda battle? To what extent was it related to the U–2 program? Would not such a procedure neglect other countries in which armaments could be manufactured and experimentation pursued for the Soviet Union just as the German army had Soviet facilities in the 1920's?

Not to be outdone by Eisenhower's and Bulganin's proposals, Eden and Faure hastened to get into the act. Eden, following his desire for minor, step-by-step agreements, advocated a specific demilitarized zone in Central Europe where joint inspection teams would operate by mutual consent, providing a practical test of the device of international inspection.

Faure wanted each nation to announce annually the amount of appropriation intended for military use. An agreed formula would then be applied by agreement to reduce the amount of

[10] *Ibid.*, 56–59; Robert J. Donovan, *Eisenhower: the Inside Story,* 345–49.

money to be spent. The funds saved would be applied towards helping needy nations.[11]

None of these proposals were seriously considered by the heads of government, but were thrust on the over-burdened foreign ministers, whose meetings had reached an impasse over a proposal for a foreign ministers meeting in October to consider the huge pile of leftovers. Surfeited by all these proposals, July 22 brought only statements by Eisenhower and Eden favoring better methods of communication, study, and travel between the two sides.

The last day of the conference was devoted to closing statements and publishing a directive for the foreign ministers who had already been quarreling over it in their meetings. The three Western leaders overflowed with generalities and platitudes befitting the occasion. Bulganin had differing views and again beat the drum for the Russian collective security agreement. Such a proposal would "relax tension and improve security." Unification of Germany was unrealistic. Once more he argued for the Soviet disarmament plan, adding that other proposals would be studied. He was unhappy that they had neglected the Far East, for there could not be any peace without solving these problems. He finished with his own platitudes about desiring peace and displaying the spirit of co-operation shown at Geneva.

The directive for the foreign ministers produced wrangling over the priority of the questions to be submitted to the foreign ministers. Eden wanted German unity first, but Bulganin argued for the security question first, disarmament second, and German unification third. Although unification and security were mentioned in the first paragraph of the directive, Bulganin won because security was to be mentioned before unification in the same paragraph. The ministers were to check on the work of the U.N. disarmament commission and study the development of East-West contacts.

[11] *Geneva*, 59–62.

This summit conference was unique because of the publicity arrangements. Wilson's dictum of "open covenants openly arrived at" (if there had been any) almost occurred. In the Maison de la Press, the old Assembly of the League of Nations building, over one thousand reporters had their choice of daily briefings from the four powers. James Hagerty, Eisenhower's press secretary, instructed the reporters on United States views. Sir George Young, head of the Foreign Office news department, described the meetings as his government saw them. Pierre Baroduc, lucid in mind and tongue, and much too fast in his explanations for the reporters, spoke for France. Leonid Ilyichev, for the Russian team, put on a dour appearance as a minor-league Molotov.

Churchill's hope for intimate talks never fully materialized. Although buffets were held after the plenary sessions, with so many people about there was small chance for private talk. Eisenhower refused all invitations to dinner except those from his Swiss hosts as a matter of protocol because he was the only chief of state present while the others were merely heads of government. The President did not go out of his way to cultivate the Soviet leaders. His only private meeting was a luncheon for Marshal Georgy Zukov on July 20. When the conversation turned to conference subjects instead of reminiscences about the war, Zhukov followed the line laid down by his superiors. To Eisenhower, "he spoke as if he was repeating a lesson that had been drilled into him until he was letter perfect."[12]

With Nikita Khrushchev, the party secretary and the most important Russian present, Eisenhower had no private talks although he perceived Khrushchev's importance before the conference ended. Eisenhower's advisers should have insisted more on the realities of the Soviet system, and protocol should not have stood in the way of confidential talks with the first secretary of the Communist Party of the U.S.S.R.

The Soviet leaders labored to project a new image. They

[12] Eisenhower, *Mandate for Change*, 524–25; *New York Times*, July 20, 1955.

drove around Geneva in open cars waving to the crowds like American politicians running hard for re-election. In contrast, Eisenhower rode about the city in a closed Cadillac sedan, followed by carloads of Secret Service men. Whenever he alighted, the Secret Service agents immediately formed a hard-muscled guard.

"It's just like gangsters!" one Swiss citizen exclaimed.[13]

The summit conference revealed basic differences in the Western attitudes confronting the Russians. Eisenhower favored talking in generalities. Three times in the afternoon of July 20 he mentioned building bridges between the East and West, with reference to the need for friendship and a new spirit. His desire for appeasement, in the original Chamberlain sense, alarmed many in Europe.

Eden and Faure produced detailed plans of limited scope while the Soviet leader proposed a definite security pact and a disarmament plan. Eisenhower advocated a plan that had slight chance of Congressional approval. The Russian leaders could have accepted some form of open-skies inspection and an exchange of blueprints; then they could have watched the battle in the United States where Eisenhower would have been pitted against his own party.

Eisenhower's tactics, certainly approved by Dulles, involved expressions of boundless good will which alone were incapable of bridging basic clashes between Soviet and Western interests. Realities of power would have been perhaps more convincing because platitudes meant little and were insufficient in such important problems.

Eisenhower's reluctance to be specific was a remnant of the ghost of the Yalta and Potsdam conferences. Because specific agreements had been made which were unsuccessful, Eisenhower would make none in Geneva. In contrast to this, he used the slap-on-the-shoulder, "how's the wife and kids?" technique which was standard operating procedure in a salesman's con-

[13] *Time*, August 1, 1955, p. 16.

vention where the problems were not as grim as those facing the Geneva Summit Conference.

Western leaders were hampered by their dislike for the chief idea of the other delegations. Faure's seemed too impractical and open to evasion. Eden's plan did not suit the French who remembered inspection troubles in Korea and the Rhineland before 1936. Eisenhower had not consulted his colleagues on the open-skies plan, and they thought it vague and impractical. The Americans and their German allies objected to Eden's plan because it would stabilize the territorial *status quo* in Germany and give implicit recognition to the existing division.

The trio failed to agree on any one plan behind which they could unite their efforts. Because Western disunity was so obvious, the Soviet leaders had no difficulty in rejecting three different plans.

Of the three plans, Eisenhower's open-skies project was the most spectacular and caught the fancy of Western public opinion. Those who formulated this idea were naïve indeed if they imagined that Soviet leaders would ever have considered negotiating the proposal. With secrecy so important to the Soviet system, Bulganin and Khrushchev might have been overthrown if they had contemplated negotiating away the jealously guarded secrecy. Because the open-skies plan was so startling and impossible to negotiate, it smacked too much of the crudest propaganda. Realizing it could never be set up, the American delegation presented it to score publicity points.

Before the Supreme Soviet on August 4, Bulganin rejected Eisenhower's open-skies plan. Nevertheless, he called the Geneva meeting a success because it had laid the foundations for a restoration of the old wartime partnership and contributed to lessening international tensions. The personal contact was fruitful, Bulganin declared, indicating an improvement in relations between the great powers. [14]

For the Russians, the conference revealed that the West

[14] *New York Times,* August 5, 1955.

was unwilling to go to war over Central Europe. The conference may have persuaded Khrushchev that intervention in the Middle East was possible. Too much time was spent by Eisenhower and Eden explaining how much they wanted peace at any price. Khrushchev's actions in the Middle East and Hungary in 1956 were based on what he had learned of Western desires for peace at the Geneva Conference.

Quiet, tough-minded talks might have counted for more. The four leaders, seated at large tables, addressed each other as if they were speaking on a panel at a convention. The series of statements read to the assembled delegations and the multitude of onlookers made the conference a public meeting. Such an atmosphere weakened the urgent feeling that the problems and dangers of the past decade required serious study and discussion. Before an audience there was no opportunity for negotiating.

Too much was unloaded on the foreign ministers without altering the basic facts of East-West power relations. After the commotion of a summit conference had dissipated, the heads of government turned affairs back to the men who should have handled the negotiations first if the heads of government did not intend to reach an agreement.

At the Geneva Conference, the Soviet government did not share the feeling that the West bargained from strength. The Russians stated their demands without offering anything in return. There was no hesitation in clarifying their goals: end NATO, rid Europe of American troops, maintain the *status quo* in Central and Eastern Europe. German unification was possible only on Russian terms.

True negotiation of the German question was difficult because London and Washington had promised German Chancellor Konrad Adenauer that his wishes would be followed. Adenauer rejected neutralization of Germany, restriction of the actions of any future German government, and discussion of the treaties which had bestowed independence on West Germany.

From a Swiss villa, Adenauer encouraged Dulles in these policies.[15]

The four leaders never seriously tried to negotiate by putting forward proposals which they thought had any chance of agreement. The quartet dealt only in generalities and propaganda, each trying to outpoint the other in publicity. Much was referred to the foreign ministers, and there generalities ceased; reality took over. The Cold War continued.

The results of Geneva were meager. Russian leaders learned that war would not come over German unification. The Western powers were unwilling to liberate the east European satellites if war was the price of freedom.

To the West came the realization that the Russian leaders were more interested in destroying NATO and in hastening Western disarmament than in unifying Germany through free elections. For the present, Russia wanted the *status quo* in Germany. The American delegation was determined to uphold the interests of Konrad Adenauer and his West German government. Russian attitude on the German problem pushed the American delegation into a consideration of walking out of the conference. Hoping that something might be achieved on paper in the final moments of the conference, however, the Americans remained.[16]

In his memoirs, Eisenhower judged the Geneva Conference a "limited success." He claimed that "in spite of what happened thereafter, the cordial atmosphere of the talks, dubbed the 'Spirit of Geneva,' never faded entirely." From this conference, he maintained, came also the exchange visits of American and Russian scientists and musicians, and the more publicized visits of Anastas Mikoyan, Frol Kozlov, and the famous trip of Richard Nixon to Moscow where he argued with Khrushchev over refrigerators.[17] Never did Eisenhower define the "Spirit of Geneva." Bulganin and Khrushchev referred to it often without any definition.

---

[15] Charles Wighton, *Adenauer. A Critical Biography*, 222–23.
[16] Eisenhower, *Mandate for Change*, 524.   [17] *Ibid.*, 530.

Bulganin revealed one result of the conference sometime later at a diplomatic reception. Ignoring champagne and vodka, he took a dry Martini. He cried: "We opened a new road to the solution of international problems at Geneva. It was there that President Eisenhower introduced us to the dry martini."[18]

The conference should have been used for exploration of Russian intentions regarding their disarmament plans of May 10 and July 21. Perhaps the face-to-face confrontation desired by Churchill might have been more effective in exploring how far the Soviet leaders would go.

Throughout the conference United States leaders were fearful of the ghosts of summit conferences past, which had been used for political ammunition in Eisenhower's presidential election campaign, and these fears prevented more definite accomplishments. Feeling that too much had been decided in the past, nothing must be decided now. When Eisenhower returned to the United States, Vice-President Richard M. Nixon was so frightened of the comparison with the Munich Conference of 1938 that he banned umbrellas at the airport reception. To quiet the ghosts of Munich, Eisenhower made his arrival speech standing in the rain.

The four powers never seriously intended to reach agreement. For the United States, Dulles made it quite plain before he left for Geneva on July 13, "The Geneva Conference will be a beginning and not an end. It is not to be expected that great decisions of substance will be made there."[19] He was correct.

If Churchill originally intended a confrontation and an exploration of the ideas and views of the Soviet leaders, this was not achieved. Nor was there serious negotiation because that had never been desired. The conference was a new departure in diplomacy in creating a new vehicle for propaganda. Leaders issued statements which news correspondents raced to flash

[18] Charles Roetter, *The Diplomatic Art. An Informal History of World Diplomacy*, 235–36.
[19] *Geneva*, 12.

around the world. No summit conference in history had so consciously sought to make headlines; neither had any conference been so successful in swapping pious platitudes.

The correspondents, the diplomats, and the heads of government departed from Geneva. They had left the world much as it had been before. They could have done worse.

12

A Conference for Khrushchev

B EFORE the next summit conference, Nikita Khrushchev battled his way up to the top of the Soviet hierarchy. An ex-sheepherder and steelworker, with a limited technical education, he found his career in the Communist Party machinery. By 1934, he had become first secretary of the Communist Party in the Moscow city organization, entering the Politburo in 1939. He survived Stalin's purges and when necessary purged those who had earned Stalin's suspicion. During World War II he commanded Ukrainian guerrillas behind German lines; in 1944, he returned to restore Communist rule in the Ukraine. On the eve of Stalin's death, Khrushchev, a true "Stalin-man," had a seat on the Presidium of the Central Committee, and he was also a member of the Party Secretariat. By September 1953, he had become the first secretary of the Communist Party. Using this powerful office as his base, he fought off his rivals, denounced Stalin, mended his political fences and pushed those forward who would help his career. The cocky, rotund party careerist became premier of the U.S.S.R. in 1958. Loud-mouthed, shrewd, and if need be, vicious, Khrushchev was premier because he had survived and won in one of the most ruthless modern political systems.

He had a new conception of the summit conference. No longer would it be discreetly discussed or carefully prepared, but whenever there came a change in the diplomatic barometer, Khrushchev immediately announced the need for a summit conference. To him it had become a device for exploiting East-West differences instead of quieting them. For Western statesmen his exploitation of the summit conference was revolutionary and irritating; for people desiring peace, it was tragic.

When the Suez crisis came in November 1956, the president of Switzerland proposed a summit conference, fearing a third world war. Moscow took up the invitation but Eisenhower refused, preferring to turn the matter over to the United Nations.

When the next summit call came, the balance of power had been altered; on October 4, 1957, the first Sputnik roared off into the Siberian skies. Speaking to the Supreme Soviet on November 6, Khrushchev called for a high-level meeting to reach an agreement on the armaments race, peaceful coexistence, and settlement by negotiations. In a long letter to Eisenhower, Bulganin announced in December that Khrushchev and he were willing to have another meeting to discuss nuclear testing. Before Eisenhower could reply, another call was sent forth by Moscow January 8, 1958, for a meeting of the heads of government of NATO countries, the Warsaw Pact members, India, Afghanistan, Egypt, Yugoslavia, Sweden, Austria, and Communist China. The meetings should open within two to three months in Geneva without preliminary consultation of the foreign ministers. The Soviet announcement contained a variety of problems for discussion:

ending of nuclear tests, renunciation of the use of atomic weapons, agreement on a free zone in central Europe, nonaggression pact between the NATO and Warsaw Pact members, withdrawal of foreign troops from Germany, discussion of means of disarmament control, expansion of international trade, agreement to end the propaganda war, China, and reductions of tension in the Middle East.[1]

Eisenhower declared on January 12 in a letter to Bulganin that personal contacts did not automatically produce good results. He was willing to go to another summit conference, but it was essential that the issues be prepared in advance, thus determining if there were any hopes that the meeting would help the cause of peace.[2]

Secretary of State Dulles reiterated these views on January 16, declaring that a stroke of the pen would not end the Cold War. A summit conference would only divert the free people from the needed effort. The meeting must be well prepared; there must be assurances that important topics would be discussed and that prospects for agreement were good. He theorized that Khrushchev was calling the meeting in an effort to create discontent among the peoples of the free world who would object to increased taxes, large armament costs, and economic assistance programs. Dulles feared that when the heads of government met they would be under great pressure "to come out with something or have a break." He did not want them to be in that condition until a worthwhile agreement was possible. There was no value in a new summit meeting that did not consider the reunification of Germany through free elections, "the one subject that was agreed on at the last summit meeting and treat that as washed up." He asserted: "If we treat agreements at the 'summit' as of no future significance, and their only purpose is to have a meeting to seem to agree, have the

---

[1] Soviet Proposals, January 8, 1958, Department of State, *Background of Heads of Government Conference, 1960* (hereafter cited as *Background*), 117–29.
[2] *Ibid.,* 129–38.

agreement violated and then start another meeting on another topic, I can't imagine a worse course of procedure or one that would be more disastrous."[3]

Khrushchev continued his campaign with a speech at Minsk on January 22, 1958. The Soviet Union wanted the summit conference because only a "calm and reasonable settlement" of the present troubles could bring peace. "As for us champions of peace, we want to hold a summit meeting without delay in order to solve all urgent problems—provided of course, there is willingness on both sides, and thereby to create a certain atmosphere of warmth in relations between states." For this summit conference to succeed, there must be recognition of the principles of peaceful coexistence and there should not be any interference in affairs of other nations. He opposed the discussion of the German question, let the Germans solve it themselves; nor would he have Eisenhower, Dulles, and Konrad Adenauer discuss the "people's democracies in eastern Europe."[4]

In a letter to Eisenhower on February 1, Bulganin argued that a foreign ministers meeting prior to the heads of government meeting would create obstacles because of the "prejudiced position of some of the possible participants." The only preparation for the conference was an agreement to meet, then the other questions could be answered.[5]

Later that month, Eisenhower complained that Khrushchev refused to discuss topics such as Eastern Europe at the summit conference but freely talked about them in his speech at Minsk. Again Eisenhower insisted on preliminary talks between ambassadors and foreign ministers, but he admitted that the United States government was considering the prospects of a summit meeting with other nations.[6]

The Soviet leaders hastened to inform the world officially

[3] Replies to questions at the National Press Club, January 16, 1958, *ibid.*, 139–42.
[4] *Ibid.*, 142–52.
[5] *Ibid.*, 153–62.
[6] Eisenhower to Bulganin, February 15, 1958, *ibid.*, 162–68.

on February 28 that they were ready for a foreign ministers meeting in April to prepare for a summit conference. Invitations to the meeting would be dispatched to all the NATO countries, the Warsaw Pact members, India, Afghanistan, Egypt, Yugoslavia, Sweden, and Austria. If that list were too long, they would be happy to include only the foreign ministers from the United States, Great Britain, France, Italy, the U.S.S.R., Poland, Czechoslovakia, Rumania, India, Yugoslavia, and Sweden. A long list of possible topics for the summit conference was proposed including cessation of testing of atomic weapons, a non-aggression pact, reduction of foreign troops in Europe, lessening of tension, and a German peace treaty. Questions relating to internal affairs, particularly Eastern Europe, would not be considered by the Soviet government at any summit meeting.[7]

The United States government replied on March 6 with the question: Was this to be a spectacle or a meeting for "meaningful decisions?" If the latter, there must be advance preparation. The conference must be a continuation of the 1955 Geneva meeting with the same problems for discussion. This answer reflected the thinking of John Foster Dulles, who rejected the Soviet terms that there could be no agreement without a prior summit meeting. Although he was willing to work for an understanding with the Soviet government, he was suspicious of another summit meeting in order to achieve agreement. "We have made a lot of agreements with the Russians and some of them have stood up and others have been broken," he declared on March 13. "But the agreements that have stood up the best were not made at the summit meeting." He found no magic in a summit meeting and considered the Soviet government unreasonable to demand: "We are not going to be willing to do what is in the interests of mankind unless it is done at the summit." From the Russians, he wanted serious talk on significant topics in advance of any summit meeting. To Dulles, these included the reunifica-

[7] *Aide memoire*, February 28, 1958, ibid., 168–71.

Nikita S. Khrushchev, center, facing camera, held an impromptu press conference outside the Russian Embassy in Paris on May 17, 1960. He informed newspaper correspondents that there would be no summit conference unless President Eisenhower apologized for the U–2 Affair and publicly admitted U.S. "aggression against the Soviet People." On the preceding day at a preliminary session, President Eisenhower had assured Khrushchev that there would be no other U–2 flights over the Soviet Union.

Courtesy Wide World Photos

After "torpedoing" what would have been the Paris Summit Conference of 1960, Premier Khrushchev clowns with a French wood chopper at Pleurs, France, about sixty miles east of Paris.

Courtesy Wide World Photos

tion of Germany and the conditions in the countries of Eastern Europe; they did not include Asia and the Middle East.[8]

On March 31, 1958, the three Western powers agreed to a summit conference preceded by preparatory work through regular channels and a foreign ministers meeting to decide on the date, place, and composition of the summit meeting. But the Soviet leaders wanted the questions considered by the ambassadors kept to a minimum, and if the foreign ministers failed to reach full agreement the summit conference would still meet. The Soviet government was ready to begin an exchange of views in Moscow on April 17.

On that date the three Western ambassadors, Maurice de Jean, Sir Patrick Reilly, and Llewellyn Thompson, called on Soviet foreign minister Andrei Gromyko, who alleged that he was unprepared to receive them together but would meet with each individually. Later he complained that three NATO ambassadors and one Warsaw Pact minister was unfair! If they wanted a conference of ambassadors, then he needed the support of the Polish and Czech ambassadors.[9] The Western powers capitulated to these demands. Throughout May the meetings proceeded without leaks by the Soviet government; even Khrushchev kept quiet. Dulles admitted on May 20, "I think that it's more certain than ever before that there will be a summit meeting." By the end of the month, the Western powers were so satisfied that their ambassadors discussed with Gromyko possible topics for the summit conference.[10]

Western unity was still strong, too much so for Khrushchev. On June 11, 1958, he complained to Eisenhower that preliminary talks were not helping to convene the summit conference. On the contrary, they were making no progress. A summit con-

---

[8] *Aide memoire*, March 6, 1958, *ibid.*, 181–85; Dulles' news conference, March 13, 1958, *American Foreign Policy, Current Documents, 1958*, 767–70.

[9] *Aide memoire*, April 26, 1958, *Background*, 206–208.

[10] News conference, May 20, 1958, *American Foreign Policy, Current Documents, 1958*, 800; *New York Times*, June 3, 1958.

ference, he insisted, ought to "ease relations between states, to liquidate the cold war, to insure conditions of peaceful coexistence of states." If the Western powers were not prepared to find a solution to all the problems proposed by the Soviet Union, then the Western leaders ought to select some topics from the list, and then they could reach agreement on these. He complained that new questions were being raised which made agreement more impossible. Why did they continue to bring up Eastern Europe? Russia had relations with these nations and found no tensions. According to Khrushchev, the demand of the West that German unification be studied was only another means to avoid the summit conference. It was time to ask, "Do all the parties really wish a summit conference to be convened?" He wanted to know if the Western powers were serious in their intentions to organize a summit conference.[11] The negotiations collapsed on June 16 when Khrushchev released some of the correspondence with Eisenhower.

Khrushchev probably found that the Western nations were tying him down to conditions and seeking to limit his maneuverability at the conference table. He wanted a summit conference just to have one; he had no intention to settle the questions desired by the West. The British and Americans insisted on placing Germany and Eastern Europe on the agenda. For Khrushchev, the moment was ill suited for a summit conference.

A more propitious occasion came when President Eisenhower dispatched American troops to Lebanon and Syria in 1958. Now Khrushchev could call the conference and force the Western powers to discuss the questions that were embarrassing to them. On July 19, he damned the "armed intervention" of the British and American troops as an old trick of the imperialists and warned that the aggressors were playing with fire. Because peace and war hung in the balance, the Soviet Union could no longer remain aloof. He proposed a conference of the heads of government of the U.S.S.R., the United States, Great Britain,

[11] *Background,* 238–49.

France, and India, along with the secretary general of the United Nations. They would take "urgent measures to stem the beginning military conflict . . . . We propose to meet on any day, at any hour, the sooner the better."[12]

In his reply on July 22, Eisenhower mentioned the possibility of having a summit conference in the United Nations Security Council. Under the terms of the United Nations Charter the heads of government and their foreign ministers could represent their nations in the Security Council. Khrushchev speedily assented, but he wanted Jawaharlal Nehru, prime minister of India, to attend. Eisenhower objected because Khrushchev was seeking to alter the composition of the Security Council. The President desired the permanent representatives to consider the proposal first, but Khrushchev objected as did the new President of France, Charles de Gaulle. Such a meeting would increase the prestige of an international organization for which De Gaulle had no affection; he suggested a meeting of the heads of government in Europe. Khrushchev concurred, suggesting Moscow as the site. He accused Eisenhower of trying to bury the summit conference by his insistence on going first to the Security Council. On August 1, Eisenhower informed Khrushchev that he had instructed the United States permanent representative at the United Nations to bring up the question of a special meeting of the heads of government in the Security Council on August 12 in New York. He rejected Moscow for a meeting place because of recent well-organized demonstrations over the Middle East outside the American embassy.

Khrushchev suddenly reversed his position and settled for a special meeting of the General Assembly of the United Nations for August 8–21. Objections from the Chinese Communists probably brought Khrushchev's sudden change. They were most unhappy over the thought of Khrushchev sitting down at a summit conference called in the Security Council. If leaders of the nations represented on the Security Council met in a summit

12 Khrushchev to Eisenhower, July 19, 1958, *ibid.*, 263–66.

conference, Khrushchev would have to sit down with Chiang Kai-shek.

The next call for a summit conference came on November 10, 1958, when Khrushchev opened a new crisis by demanding the end of the occupation of Berlin and a Western agreement with the East German government. Dulles retorted with a warning that the United States government was committed to holding Berlin by force if necessary.

On November 27, the crisis warmed up with the Soviet announcement that the wartime agreements were at an end, the occupation of Berlin was unlawful, and that West Berlin must become a demilitarized free city within six months. In January, 1959, Moscow demanded a conference of all states who had fought Germany to consider a Soviet draft of a peace treaty.

In a speech before the voters of the Kalinin election district in Moscow on February 24, Khrushchev rejected any discussion on the question of German unification. That was a matter for the Germans themselves. He accused the West of seeking to draw "us into a labyrinth of diplomatic talks so that we will be involved in such talks for several years." The premier called for a meeting of the heads of government to examine the basic issues; they could begin with a German peace treaty.[13]

The United States government proposed a foreign ministers meeting on the German question with representatives of both Germanies present. The Soviet government replied that if the heads of government had been unable to settle relations how could the foreign ministers? A summit conference could further the "normalization of the whole international atmosphere." Great would be the historical significance if the heads of government decided in a summit conference that henceforward they would settle all problems on the basis of peaceful coexistence.[14]

---

[13] *American Foreign Policy, Current Documents*, 1959, 1614–1615.

[14] Notes from the Soviet Union to the United States, March 2, 1959, *Background*, 330–33.

Harold Macmillan threw his weight behind the Russian call for a summit conference. He preferred to do business with Russians at the summit because lesser officials lacked authority to bargain and make concessions. Instead of the semipublic speeches made at Geneva in 1955, he wanted the leaders to meet privately and emerge only to make statements when they had reached agreement. In March he traveled to Washington, Paris, Bonn, Ottawa, and Moscow to learn about summit possibilities.

In Moscow he promised to push for a summit conference without insisting on prior conditions. He encountered resistance when he conferred with Eisenhower who declared that he would not go to a summit meeting unless "there was evidence of good faith and some progress that promised results from a summit." Macmillan argued that World War I could have been avoided if the heads of government had held a summit conference. Instead, Sir Edward Grey, the British foreign secretary, "went fishing and the war came in which the United Kingdom lost two million young men." Eisenhower reminded him of the Munich Conference; he did not want to participate in a repetition of that. Macmillan insisted that he must attempt a summit conference regardless of the preparations. The President held out for a foreign ministers meeting to prepare the way for a summit conference. If the ministers were successful in narrowing the issues and preparing proposals for the heads of government to consider, Eisenhower would attend. Macmillan gave in to the President's demand.[15]

On March 19, Khrushchev agreed to such a meeting as a preliminary to the summit conference. He withdrew his ultimatum of November 27, admitting that the Western governments had a legal right to be in Berlin. The foreign ministers conference met May 11–June 20 in Geneva and agreed on little of importance except to take a three week recess.

Unhappy over the lack of progress at Geneva, Eisenhower

[15] Dwight D. Eisenhower, *Waging the Peace,* 354–55, 401.

decided to invite Khrushchev to the United States when he learned that the Soviet leader had expressed interest in such a journey. Eisenhower intended to tie the invitation to progress in the foreign ministers meeting which would make a summit conference possible. According to Eisenhower, his instructions were misunderstood by Under-Secretary of State Robert Murphy who delivered the invitation without conditions attached.[16] Khrushchev accepted gladly, but the foreign ministers meeting reconvened July 13 and struggled on until August 5 without any agreement on the basis for a summit conference.

When Khrushchev visited the United States in September, 1959, he argued that the time was ripe for a summit conference, and he was ready to go anywhere for a meeting. In the Camp David talks with Eisenhower, Khrushchev accepted a postponement of his Berlin demands. Eisenhower assented to a summit conference before the end of the year and accepted an invitation to visit Moscow.

Khrushchev came away from Camp David believing that he had convinced Eisenhower to be realistic and let Russia have her own way over Berlin at the summit conference. Dulles, who was dead, could no longer exert his influence over the President. Eisenhower's attitude at Geneva and his lack of initiative in the Hungarian revolt led Khrushchev to imagine that his solution for the Berlin problem would be acceptable.

Another chief of state insisted on a postponement. Charles de Gaulle, now president of the Fifth French Republic, stalled on the summit conference lest some agreement be reached there over atomic weapons before France had joined the atomic club. The General was insistent on adequate preparation before the conference met; the Russians must show by their actions that they were willing to reduce tension. He wanted to establish personal contact with Khrushchev before the meeting and invited him to come to Paris in the spring of 1960. Thus the summit conference was postponed at his insistence. Khrushchev was

16 *Ibid.*, 405–407.

overjoyed to accept the postponement because he wanted time to split the West. He could work his wiles on De Gaulle before the summit conference and soften him up while isolating the West Germans, who with De Gaulle, supported a hard policy on Berlin. Also Russian scientists could hasten their preparations for another Soviet space feat.

The Western leaders, together with Konrad Adenauer, met in Paris on December 19 to seek unity for the coming conference, but they could not find it. Macmillan wanted an interim agreement, i.e., the Western powers could offer concessions if the Russians recognized their rights and access to Berlin. The West Germans and De Gaulle were opposed. Adenauer favored postponement of a summit conference where Germany's fate would be discussed; he rejected any interim settlement on Berlin that involved a change in Western power status in Germany.[17] De Gaulle resisted close integration of the NATO forces, despite the fervent pleadings of Eisenhower. The trio could not reach any agreement on counter proposals to Khrushchev's demands on general and complete disarmament. However, they decided to invite Khrushchev to a summit conference in Paris. By the end of the year the date for the conference had been set for May 16, 1960.

In January, 1960, the Western powers appointed a committee to outline the position of the three governments for the conference, but they failed to reach a firm agreement. On March 22, Christian Herter, John Foster Dulles' successor as secretary of state, confessed that Eisenhower did not yet have an agenda. He hoped the meeting would change the Soviet attitude and lead to an agreement. The meeting would be a gamble; great results should not be expected. He told the Senate Foreign Relations Committee on April 21 that the prime objective of the Western powers at the summit conference would be to learn if the U.S.S.R. "sincerely wished to ease tensions."

As late as April the Western governments had no new ideas

17 *New York Times*, November 3, December 29, 1959.

for the meeting; they would leave the initiative in Khrushchev's hands. The French and Germans were pessimistic, but the British and United States diplomats hoped that Khrushchev would not be too tough if nothing worsened East–West relations. Some believed that he was under such pressure at home to relax tensions that he would reach some broad agreement, perhaps on disarmament, which would be hammered into a firm accord through a later agreement. Perhaps an interim agreement on Berlin might be achieved leaving Allied rights intact.[18]

Khrushchev had other ideas. During the winter and twice during his visit to France, March 23–April 2, he threatened that if no progress was reached on a settlement of the Berlin problems, the U.S.S.R. would sign a separate peace treaty with East Germany. Then Western access to Berlin would be ended.

In his talks with Khrushchev, De Gaulle maintained that the Western Powers had the right of access to Berlin. He would refuse to recognize East Germany in any reunification proposal. A State Department spokesman hastened to announce that any attempt to alter the status of Berlin without the consent of all four powers would be without legal basis. In London the British government decided to oppose any Soviet suggestion for gradually altering the status of West Berlin to that of a free city. There was no desire for a separate treaty between Russia and East Germany.

In a speech to the National Association of Broadcasters in Chicago on April 4, Secretary of State Christian A. Herter declared that German reunification should be accomplished through "free plebiscites and that a final peace settlement should be concluded with the German government formed on the basis of such plebiscites." He warned that in the summit conference the Western powers were "determined to protect the freedom and security of the people of West Berlin." The Soviet leaders must not mistake United States firmness. At the coming Paris

[18] *Ibid.*, March 23, April 16, 21, 1960.

meeting, "the west will continue to make clear the free world's determination to defend essential rights."[19]

To the AFL-CIO Conference on World Affairs on April 20, Under-Secretary of State Douglas Dillon spelled out the United States' position on Germany at the summit conference. His speech was also intended for an audience in Moscow. The United States was resolved "to maintain our presence in Berlin and to preserve its ties with the Federal Republic." Nothing would be done to abandon West Berlin or weaken freedom in West Germany. At the summit conference the United States would seek a solution of the German and Berlin problems as well as methods to improve East-West relations. Dillon advised Khrushchev and his colleagues not to assume "that we will bow to threats" or accept their "distorted" version of the German problem as the basis for negotiation.[20]

The Herter and Dillon speeches heralded a change in the United States' attitude towards the summit conference. Khrushchev's threats would encounter opposition, and his demands on Berlin and Germany would not be met. There would be no repetition of the Munich Conference as some in West Germany had feared.

Khrushchev replied in a speech at Baku on April 25. He was not enthusiastic over the coming summit conference. He accused Western statesmen of taking a one-sided line on some of the problems and singled out Dillon's speech which "reeks of the cold war spirit." From this speech he concluded that the United States was ready for agreement if its viewpoint on Berlin was accepted. This he rejected. Again he sounded the call to make West Berlin a free city and demanded a peace treaty. To continue the present situation would only preserve a "hotbed of provocations" in West Berlin. If the Western powers refused to

[19] *Ibid.*, April 5, 1960; *The Department of State Bulletin*, April 25, 1960.
[20] *New York Times*, April 21, 1960; *The Department of State Bulletin*, May 9, 1960.

sign a peace treaty with Russia, he would sign one with East Germany. If the Western powers wanted to resort to the "positions of strength" policy, Russia and other Socialist countries would match efforts and show the sterility of such a policy. The only solution was peaceful coexistence between the capitalists and socialist states. Unlike some Western leaders, he refused to reduce the summit conference to a noncommittal exchange of opinions and sheer conversation in order to avoid framing concrete solutions.[21]

Now Khrushchev knew that the Western powers' position was hardening. He had failed to scare De Gaulle with the story of German threat to France. The British were having second thoughts about Berlin. The Herter and Dillon speeches indicated a toughening in United States policy on Germany.

Khrushchev had labored for three years to have this summit conference. He wanted it for personal as well as national prestige. Already he was feeling pressure from Communist China whose leaders wanted to speak for world Communism. Khrushchev had been seduced by a wonderful propaganda opportunity: thousands of newsmen would be waiting to report his words to all mankind. His words and actions would improve his image in Russia. He had hoped that at the summit conference the West would be so frightened of his brinksmanship that they would succumb to his wishes about Berlin. Now his hopes of settling Berlin on his own terms had been destroyed, and all his labors had been in vain. He faced a summit conference that would surely fail, and he would be blamed at home and abroad.

[21] *Current Digest of the Soviet Press,* Vol. XII, No. 17, pp. 5–7.

13

The U-2

A BIZARRE SERIES of events began on May 1 which ultimately destroyed the Paris Summit Conference. A high-altitude
reconnaissance plane was shot down near Sverdlovsk, Russia,
and the pilot was captured. He was Francis Gary Powers, an
American citizen, employed by the Central Intelligence Agency.
Powers' plane, called a "U–2," was especially designed for
flight at altitudes above those of fighters and rockets and was
crammed with photographic equipment. For four years the
Central Intelligence Agency had directed U–2 flights for the
purpose of photographic observation of Russia, her satellites, and
Communist China. The project was a brilliant feat of espionage
which gave the United States government invaluable information on the Soviet Union without permitting the Russians to

photograph the United States in return as they could have done under Eisenhower's open-skies proposal.

The U–2 flights had been suspended when General Nathan F. Twining, Air Force chief of staff, visited Russia in June and July, 1956, and again when Khrushchev visited the United States in September, 1959. A successful mission had been completed on April 9, 1960, but it had not gone undetected by the Soviet armed forces. This fact was known in Washington.

Eisenhower approved another U–2 flight even though the summit conference could be endangered. There was fear lest a *détente* be reached at the Paris meeting which might lead to a permanent grounding of the U–2 planes. Because this might be the last flight, one more mission ought to be attempted. The Central Intelligence Agency had information that a new Soviet rocket rested on its launching pad near Sverdlovsk. Powers' mission would be to photograph this rocket. His flight would originate in Pakistan and end in Norway. May 1 was chosen because that was a Russian holiday, and the radar and rocket crews might be relaxed.[1]

Near Sverdlovsk Powers' plane was shot down. He ejected himself from the plane but failed to blow it up along with himself. His parachute brought him down near a state farm. Some of the workers ran to him and helped him spill the air from his parachute. Once they realized he was a foreigner, they disarmed him and turned him over to the local authorities. Before the day ended, he had been flown to Moscow for interrogation.

Too little thought had been given in Washington to the problem of a pilot being captured alive because of human or mechanical failure. The Central Intelligence Agency assumed that little of the plane would survive to be examined by Soviet intelligence because of the fragile construction of the plane and the destruction device which the pilot would detonate, killing

[1] Sanche de Gramont, *The Secret War: the Story of International Espionage since World War II*, 256, 261–62; David Wise and Thomas B. Ross, *The U–2 Affair*, 179, 259–60.

himself at the same time. John Foster Dulles believed that if the Russians ever captured a U-2 intact, they would never dare admit the fact. They would then have to confess "that for years we had been carrying on flights over their territory while they, the Soviets, had been helpless to do anything."[2]

Unfortunately for American foreign policy, Powers failed to act like a textbook spy. Because he was a highly trained pilot instead of an espionage agent, he saved his life. Enough of the plane survived the crash to give the Russians the secret of the U-2.

When Powers failed to reach Norway, a cover story was released in the United States on May 3 announcing that an Air Force research plane was missing on a weather reconnaissance mission for the National Aeronautic Space Administration from a Turkish air base. Powers had been unable to indicate exactly where his plane had gone down. He had simply disappeared thirteen hundred miles inside Russia.

On May 5, Khrushchev went before the Supreme Soviet and revealed doubts about the summit conference, complaining that Western governments were not seeking "concrete solutions," as indicated in the recent speeches of Herter, Nixon, and Dillon. The Premier was bitter over Eisenhower's announced intention to leave the Paris Summit Conference after May 22 with Nixon remaining as his substitute. If Nixon were left to represent the United States, it would be like letting "a goat guard the cabbage!"

Then he disclosed that the missing U-2 had been shot down on May 1, but he said nothing more. Powers' fate was still a mystery. Khrushchev refused to indicate the condition of the plane and its equipment. He threatened retaliation on those countries from whence the U-2 flights originated. To the deputies, now agog with surprise, Khrushchev declared that the U-2 flight was the work of "the aggressive imperialist circles in the U.S.A." which wanted to break up the conference or prevent agreement. The flight was deliberately timed for the summit con-

2 Eisenhower, *Waging the Peace*, 546.

ference in order to exert pressure and intimidate the U.S.S.R. He wondered if the West was serious in desiring to satisfy the desires of the people for peace or merely interested in playing jokes.[3] It was one of the most exciting speeches in the dull history of the Supreme Soviet.

In Washington there was confusion. The National Aeronautic Space Administration spokesman, unaware that the agency had been used for a cover, announced on May 5 that one of their planes had been on a peaceful mission in Turkey near the Russian border and had reported oxygen trouble. *Pravda* reported on May 6 that Unit N of Antiaircraft Defense, under the able direction of Sergeant V. Yagushkin, had destroyed the plane on orders from Khrushchev. But in Washington, on the same day, Lincoln White, speaking for the State Department, categorically declared that there had not been any deliberate attempt to violate Soviet frontiers.

Once more Khrushchev mounted the podium in the great hall of the Supreme Soviet on May 7 to disclose a little more about the affair. Powers had been captured alive and had talked to his captors. Khrushchev admitted that he had deliberately withheld part of the story earlier to see what the United States government would say. The flight had originated in Pakistan; Powers' oxygen supply had not failed for if it had how did the plane wander like "a runaway horse" for miles across Afghanistan and the U.S.S.R.? After the plane had been hit, the pilot had bailed out, failing to blow up his aircraft. When he was captured, a poisoned needle was discovered on his person. "What barbarism!" the premier exclaimed. His hearers responded: "Shame! Shame!" If this was a peaceful scientific mission, why, asked Khrushchev, was the pilot armed with a pistol, complete with silencer, "He was given it for an emergency—not to take air samples, however, but to blow out a man's brains." According to the Premier, Powers was given the pistol "after

[3] *The Current Digest of the Soviet Press*, Vol. XII, No. 18, p. 16.

making genuflections as they do in churches—and they call us godless atheists."[4]

In Washington after harried all-day conferences, the State Department announced that the Powers flight was justified on the need to "obtain information now concealed behind the Iron Curtain," but no one in Washington had ordered it. Another statement came forth on May 9 from Secretary of State Christian Herter that U-2 flights had been going on for four years under instructions from President Eisenhower in order to obtain intelligence. There was no declaration that the flights would cease although he expressed the hope that at the coming summit conference the heads of government would seek the means to remove the threat of war. The U-2 incident, Herter argued should emphasize the "importance to the world of an earnest attempt to achieve agreed and effective safe-guards against surprise attack and aggression."[5]

In Moscow, on May 9, Khrushchev, in a speech at the Czech embassy, declared that the flight was deliberately timed for the summit conference. He introduced a new line of thought: if the militarists in the United States committed such deeds without the knowledge of their own government, how weak that government must be! What a lack of confidence! To his hearers he explained that because force would be used to keep the Western troops out of Berlin after the German peace treaty had been signed, some leaders in the United States had decided to teach him a lesson. First there had come the April 9 flight. Khrushchev confessed that Soviet rocket forces had failed to hit the plane; they were called to task with a warning not to let it happen again. On May 1 the plane was shot down, and the American militarists' attempt to demonstrate their strength had been frustrated.[6]

Eisenhower's press conference on May 11 did not smooth

[4] *Ibid.*, 17–19.
[5] *86 Cong. 2 sess.*, Senate Committee on Foreign Relations, *Events Incident to the Summit Conference, Hearings*, 193–94.
[6] *Current Digest of the Soviet Press*, Vol. XII, No. 19, pp. 22–23.

the road to the summit conference. While defending the flights as necessary, he considered them distasteful, vital yet unfortunate. Another Pearl Harbor had to be avoided, and because of Soviet secrecy they were necessary. He had ordered the collection of information by every possible method to protect the United States and the free world against surprise attack. Now he intimated that the flights would be ended. At the Paris Summit Conference he promised to raise the question of "open skies" as the only possible solution.

The same day in Moscow, Khrushchev gave his brand of press conference. His answers had no relation to the questions; they simply gave him a chance to catch his breath. Loudly he proclaimed that the United States was a thief who had broken into the locked home of the U.S.S.R. The Americans were bestial, cowardly imperialists, except for those who had seen the truth, such as John Reed, author of *Ten Days that Shook the World.* At his death, Khrushchev said, he was a true Communist. (When Reed died, he was a disillusioned Communist).

To invite Eisenhower to Russia now would put the Premier in "a very difficult position." If Khrushchev asked the Russian people to welcome Eisenhower after the U–2 incident, they would ask, "Are you nuts?"

As for the summit conference, Khrushchev said that it did not seem necessary to put the flight on the agenda, but there would be others there, and he did "not think that two of these three approve of this aggressive, dangerous act of American brass hats." Suppose the summit conference did not take place? He declared, "Well, we have lived without it for many years, we can do so for another hundred."[7]

Already in a published, official protest to the United States government, the Russians objected to the Powers flight as an attempt by the United States to " 'open' a foreign sky." It was "a calculated U.S.A. policy" to violate Soviet frontiers with air-

[7] *86 Cong. 2 sess.,* Senate Committee on Foreign Relations, *Events Incident to the Summit Conference, Hearings,* 203–11.

planes. Through such national policy, the Russian government insisted, the Americans sought to heat up the Cold War and "to poison the international situation before the summit meeting." The United States Department of State cynically had announced that these "provocative invasions" would continue for purposes of intelligence. If there were similar provocations, the U.S.S.R. would take retaliatory measures.

In reply, the United States government admitted that it had been collecting intelligence but only for purely defensive purposes. It denied its policy was aggressive. Never had it intended by the U–2 flights to "prejudice the success of the forthcoming meeting of heads of government in Paris." There had been no intention to heat up the Cold War.[8]

Khrushchev arrived at Orly airfield on May 14 although the conference would not officially begin until the afternoon of May 17. May 15, Eisenhower arrived in the morning, and Macmillan came about noon. Accompanied by Andrei Gromyko, the Soviet foreign minister, and Marshal Rodion I. Malinovsky, Soviet defense minister, Khrushchev called on President Charles de Gaulle. There he raged for over an hour and a half; his shouting became so loud that De Gaulle had to ask him to lower his voice. Khrushchev left a memorandum with De Gaulle setting forth the conditions which Eisenhower must meet before the Russian premier would attend the summit conference. Next, the Russian trio called on Macmillan where Khrushchev again read his memorandum. By acquainting De Gaulle and Macmillan with his complaints, Khrushchev sought to drive them into pressuring Eisenhower to give way.

After De Gaulle supplied the American delegation with a copy of Khrushchev's memorandum, Eisenhower and his delegation hastened to study the Russian position. They agreed that there was no point in arguing or quarreling but rather to use restraint and dignity in announcing that the U–2 flights had already been suspended, a fact that was not publicly known.

[8] *Ibid.*, 195–98, 211–12.

That evening at De Gaulle's invitation, Eisenhower conferred with him and Macmillan over Khrushchev's note. De Gaulle and Macmillan were sympathetic towards Eisenhower's plight. He insisted that although espionage was unpleasant, the state of American intelligence was so poor that he had no alternative. In the summit conference, however, Eisenhower stated that he would not be intimidated to "raise my hand and swear that we would never again do anything in the field of espionage." For one summit conference, he would not shackle the United States permanently.[9]

When Secretary of Defense Thomas Gates learned of the content of Khrushchev's memorandum, he ordered a combat readiness and communications alert during the night of May 15 and 16. Supposedly it was a "quiet alert," but soon the word was out in the American defense system that there was "an alert." The expected confusion and alarm occurred. Later the Defense Department alleged that it was merely a test of high-speed military communications from overseas, as well as the alert status of the military forces in all commands.[10]

On the eve of the 1960 summit conference, the omens for success were poor. An American reconnaissance plane had penetrated Russian air space bringing accusations and denials. The Eisenhower administration had been caught in a lie, and the United States Air Force was on an alert status. Now a peaceful meeting could become a major confrontation between heads of state. Serious negotiations would be difficult and meaningful results impossible. To avoid disaster, calm, effective diplomacy was required. Not since 1938 had a summit conference met amid so great a crisis.

[9] Eisenhower, *Waging the Peace*, 554.
[10] *New York Times*, May 17, 1960; Wise and Ross, *The U–2 Affair*, 146–47.

14

Paris Again, 1960

O N THE MORNING of May 16, the four heads of government and a few associates entered the Elysée Palace to confer in a room once used by Madame Pompadour, Louis XV's mistress, to receive her intimate friends. Khrushchev arrived first accompanied by Gromyko and Malinovsky. He specifically asked if they might come; later this led to speculation that they were there to check on his performance. Next came Macmillan, and then Eisenhower who entered the Elysée Palace precisely at 11:00 A.M. As host, De Gaulle escorted Eisenhower into the room. Macmillan greeted the President, but Khrushchev remained seated at the conference table. The atmosphere was cold in the charming eighteenth-century room.

De Gaulle explained that he had informed the others of

Khrushchev's position. Did anyone have anything to say? Khrushchev said, "Yes!"

In response to De Gaulle's question, the three leaders said that they would have statements to make. De Gaulle turned to Eisenhower, who was the only chief of state present.

"We shall hear from the President of the United States."

Khrushchev interrupted, "I have something to say." Ignoring protocol, the Soviet premier launched forth. He rehearsed once more the tale of the U–2 flights. Using adjectives "treacherous," "aggressive," Khrushchev seized on the clumsy manner of handling the statements to the press. He pounded away at the statements of Eisenhower, confirming that the flights over the Soviet lands had been and continued to be "the calculated policy" of the United States government personally approved by Eisenhower. How then could leaders of the four governments confer, negotiate, and consider world problems when the United States government and Eisenhower, the President, "have not only failed to condemn this provocative act . . . but on the contrary, have declared that such actions will continue to be state policy of the United States with regard to the Soviet Union." Khrushchev warmed up to his major theme. How could agreements be achieved to ease tensions and to end mistrust and suspicion when one of the great powers announces flatly "that its policy is intrusion into the territory of another great power with espionage and sabotage purposes?" Such a policy, Khrushchev argued, "dooms the summit conference to complete failure in advance." For the future, the Soviet armed forces, Khrushchev warned, would shoot down all such intruders. Those states who were accomplices of the United States in espionage and sabotage would not escape blows in the future. How could they ignore the threat of the United States to continue to fly over Soviet territory, violating "a sacred and immutable principle of international relations?"

For the conference to be successful, all powers represented must declare that "they will not undertake any actions against one another which amount to violations of the state sovereignty of the powers." Consequently, if the United States wanted to keep peace and maintain confidence between states, it must "condemn the inadmissable, provocative actions of the United States air force with regard to the Soviet Union, and secondly, refrain from continuing such actions and such a policy against the U.S.S.R. in the future."

Khrushchev demanded that Eisenhower "call to strict account those who are directly guilty of the deliberate violation by American aircraft of the state borders of the U.S.S.R." Until these demands were complied with, there was "no possibility for productive negotiations with the United States government at the summit conference." If Eisenhower would meet these demands, Khrushchev would be prepared to take part in the conference and to work for its success. Without these concessions, Khrushchev refused to meet in conference under threat of "aggressive reconnaissance flights" made because "the United States has no desire to reach a settlement." Time should elapse before the summit conference met again, perhaps six to eight months.

Then he addressed himself to the American people, whom he was convinced desired peace. Only "a small frantic group in the Pentagon" and those who would benefit from an armaments race wanted war. He thanked De Gaulle and Macmillan for their efforts in behalf of the conference. His only words directed towards Eisenhower were to withdraw the invitation to visit the Soviet Union.

In a quiet voice, Eisenhower answered with a short statement that the United States' activities were not aggressive but defensive in nature. Their purpose was to "assure the safety of the United States and the free world against surprise attack by a power which boasts of its ability to devastate the United States and other countries by missiles armed with atomic warheads." He denied that the United States had threatened to continue the flights. The flights had been suspended and would not be resumed. Eisenhower argued that he had come to Paris to seek agreements to eliminate the need for such flights, and he saw no reason for the U–2 incident to disrupt the conference. If they could not deal with the problem in Paris, he planned to introduce a proposal for a United Nations aerial surveillance force to detect preparations for attack.

Khrushchev asked if the flights would be resumed after the conference. Eisenhower replied that they were ended. Khrushchev was not satisfied. Unless the United States renounced its actions, apologized, and punished those responsible, his government would not attend the conference.

De Gaulle reminded the Soviet leader that such incidents resulted from tensions that the summit conference had been called to solve. The incident, now past, highlighted the need for them to get to work, because in the near future satellites would open up the skies in all countries. He reminded Khrushchev of the Soviet satellite launched on May 15 which was crossing France eighteen times a day.

Khrushchev swore that as God was his witness, there were no cameras in Sputnik. De Gaulle reminded him of the camera in a satellite which had photographed the far side of the moon. However, France had nothing to hide if anyone wanted to fly freely over the nation. Khrushchev replied that like De Gaulle he would allow his allies to fly over the Soviet Union. De Gaulle retorted that he meant anyone. Khrushchev yelled that he did not care "a damn about overflights."[1] Once more he demanded that the United States government through a public announcement suspend these flights, condemn them, and express regret.

Macmillan argued that espionage was a form of violating sovereignty, and it was an "unpleasant fact of life." He pointed out that the announcement of the suspension of the flights removed any threat to Soviet security. The President's announcement of the ending of the U–2 flights meant that the conference would not occur under a threat. He was glad that Khrushchev

[1] Wise and Ross, *The U–2 Affair*, 156.

did not desire the end of the conference but its postponement. He begged the others to continue the conference because the hopes of the world rested on it.

De Gaulle proposed a day's recess to seek a compromise. Khrushchev announced that he did not consider the session as the summit conference but only a preliminary meeting to decide if a conference would be held. He would issue his statement to the press, ignoring pleas from De Gaulle and Macmillan to keep the meeting confidential. Because it was only a preliminary talk, he claimed the right to inform the press. Khrushchev departed and the meeting broke up. As Eisenhower was leaving, De Gaulle said: "Whatever happens, we are with you."[2]

Throughout the meeting there had not been any informal exchange between Eisenhower and Khrushchev. They entered without a word of greeting and departed without a handshake. Macmillan tried vainly to save the conference, meeting separately later that same day with De Gaulle, Eisenhower, and finally Khrushchev. To the Soviet leader, Macmillan insisted that his fears and demands had been met for the most part. Eisenhower had given him a categorical assurance, and it had now been made public. Was he not unreasonable to demand more? Khrushchev would not be moved.

When the three Western leaders met again the next afternoon at 3:00 P.M. for the formal meeting of the summit conference, Khrushchev was absent. Sergei M. Kudryavtsev, a minister-counselor, had phoned shortly before the meeting began to ask if this were still a preliminary meeting. If so, the Premier would come. If this were the summit conference, he would come only when his three ultimatums were fulfilled. At 3:20 P.M. he phoned again to inquire about the type of meeting. De Gaulle's aide asked for a formal reply in writing to the invitation, but it was refused. The three waiting statesmen were informed at

[2] In describing this meeting, I have relied on: *New York Times; 86 Cong. 2 sess.*, Senate Committee on Foreign Relations, *Events Incident to the Summit Conference, Hearings;* Wise and Ross, *The U-2 Affair,* Eisenhower, *Waging the Peace.*

4:15 P.M. that Khrushchev had announced to the press that he would confer only after the United States government had fulfilled his conditions. The meeting adjourned at 5:00 P.M. Khrushchev had been out riding about the French countryside, stopping to swill wine with the Frenchmen and yell *"Vive la paix!"*

The Western trio waited patiently in hopes that he might relent. At 9:15 P.M. they issued a statement declaring that Khrushchev's attitude had made it impossible to open the conference.

After formal calls on De Gaulle and Macmillan on May 18, Khrushchev held his famous press conference. Before hundreds of press correspondents, he shouted, screamed, and pounded the table; he was a crude Russian peasant roaring obscenities at the "lackeys of imperialism." The summit conference, called to deal with matters of life and death, had become a circus.

Why did Khrushchev torpedo the summit conference for which he had labored so long? Amid the abundance of theories, probably no single answer is certain. Khrushchev's Baku speech suggests that he did not then intend to destroy the conference. It signified his chagrin at failing to break Allied unity. Probably he planned to go on with the conference, hoping to extract whatever propaganda he possibly could from it. The Powers flight changed his plans.

Although the U–2 flights were known to the Soviet government, their immense value to United States military intelligence could not be grasped until a plane with cameras and exposed film had fallen into Russian hands. Khrushchev and his generals must have been shocked to learn how much information the U–2 planes gave to the Central Intelligence Agency.

Should they then reveal the existence of the downed plane and the pilot's capture? Often in counterespionage more is to be gained by concealing knowledge of the enemy's method of operation. Enemy agents can then be more easily captured. In the case of the U–2, secrecy would not stop flights; it would have been impossible to cover all of Russia with rocket batteries. Not all of the U–2 flights would come within range of a Soviet rocket battery as had Powers' plane. The flights had to be stopped to preserve the secrecy of Russian progress in armaments.

The incident offered tempting propaganda opportunities. More could be gained by exploiting the U–2 flight than by plodding through a summit conference which offered little hope of success. Those mad imperialists, the evil men of the Pentagon and the Central Intelligence Agency, had sent off these flights to ruin the summit conference and spy on honest Russian citizens. "They've pulled a Forrestal," Khrushchev gleefully exclaimed.[3]

If Khrushchev could get an abject apology from Eisenhower, his prestige victory would be immense. He may have thought that after revealing his memorandum to Macmillan and De Gaulle on May 15, they would rush to pressure Eisenhower into begging forgiveness. Once he had revealed the story of the flight, however, Khrushchev did not dare let the United States get away easily, or else he would destroy the great-power symbolism of the Soviet Union. He was thus forced to threaten those nations who had allowed their facilities to be used for the U–2 flights; by threatening them he could weaken the influence of the United States. For the future, these nations would not dare permit the United States the use of their facilities lest Khrushchev be offended. Khrushchev was forced to torpedo the summit conference to satisfy the Stalinists who would always press for a tough attitude.

The Paris fiasco also belonged to the Sino-Russian dispute over pre-eminence in the Communist world. Chinese Communist sources had denounced the Paris Summit Conference because it ill befitted their position that war with the imperialist United States was inevitable and welcome. The U–2 affair offered Khrushchev an opportunity to show his Chinese critics

[3] *Current Digest of the Soviet Press,* Vol. XII, No. 22 p. 5.

how tough he could act with the Americans either by forcing an abject apology from Eisenhower or by breaking up the conference.

A struggle for power within the Kremlin in early May probably affected the summit conference.[4] On May 4 a sudden meeting of the Central Committee of the Communist Party was followed by a shakeup in the party hierarchy including the important Party Secretariat. "Kremlinologists" do not yet know the full meaning of the events of May 4, but the upheaval does indicate differences over Soviet policy growing out of the U–2 affair. In an effort to thresh out differences over policy, there were long conferences in the Kremlin between May 11 and 14.

In his first speeches after May 1, Khrushchev avoided casting all the blame for the incident on Eisenhower. He may have hoped that before the conference opened Eisenhower would apologize publicly, condemn those responsible, and announce the end of the U–2 flights. With the President then on the defensive, Khrushchev might rally De Gaulle and Macmillan to his side. When Eisenhower accepted full responsibility without ending the flights, the Kremlin leaders decided that Khrushchev should wreck the conference if Eisenhower did not fulfill Russian demands.

There was a chance for Khrushchev to win a diplomatic victory at the conference. When Eisenhower promised to end the U–2 flights, Khrushchev should have dropped his demand for an apology and made a great show of a generous concession. The Soviet leader would then have appeared more interested in peace than in heating up the Cold War.

Espionage in peacetime is normal. The United States was unfortunately caught at a most inopportune time. The May 1 flight should never have occurred if the United States government wanted to appear sincere in going to the summit conference. Khrushchev would not have been so quick to reveal

[4] Wolfgang Leonhard, *The Kremlin Since Stalin*, 359–66.

Powers' capture without means to exploit it at a summit conference. The U–2 flights might have continued and perhaps more information would have been obtained. That the Central Intelligence Agency could have been permitted to launch a flight at a time of great significance in United States foreign policy revealed lack of control by the executive branch of the government over intelligence-gathering agencies.

Allan Dulles, then C. I. A. (Central Intelligence Agency) chief, defended the confusion in the statements after May 1 by arguing that the U–2 was not like an ordinary spy because too many people knew about the plane, its purposes, and accomplishments. A plane, flown by a highly skilled technician and loaded with intricate photographic equipment, could not be handled like a secret agent caught trying to sneak across a frontier. Dulles contended that the President had to take responsibility for this; he could not thrust the blame off on a subordinate.[5]

In trying to defend his actions, Dulles overlooked the impending summit conference. Never was there a worse time for the President to be forced to take responsibility for an espionage affair, no matter how many may have been informed of the mission. If anyone should have been responsible for the U–2, that would have been the chief of the C.I.A. who would have to be sacrificed.

Dulles considered that one more flight was so important that it should take precedence over foreign policy. His attitude revealed how much American policy had come under the control of the technicians and escaped from the executive branch of government.

Those people who directed the U–2 missions were too concerned with the plane and its unique equipment as an instrument for successful espionage. They failed to ponder the possible effect on a summit conference if a plane came down and the pilot survived. In Washington, the U–2 no longer served

---

[5] Allan Dulles, *The Craft of Intelligence*, 197–98.

American foreign policy. Instead national policy was endangered for the sake of the U–2. Intelligence gathering had become important for its own sake.

Eisenhower confessed that when he personally approved of the flight plan, along with a number of others, he had no thought of its possible bearing upon the Paris Summit Conference. He contended that it would have had none if the mission succeeded.[6] Was a U–2 flight on May 1 worth the risks of endangering the summit conference less than three weeks distant? Either Eisenhower had lost control over the U–2 program or he followed faulty advice.

The United States needed to learn the value of silence in espionage. Too many people talked too much and were caught far from the truth. They would have done well to follow the example of the Macmillan government in the case of Commander Lionel Crabbe, a British agent, who disappeared in Plymouth harbor during the visit of Bulganin and Khrushchev to Britain in 1956. Officially the matter is still under investigation.

Eisenhower judged the "issuance of a premature and erroneous cover story" as the greatest error in the crisis. He ignored his role in permitting a U–2 flight across the Soviet Union when a summit conference was about to convene. He refused to cast the blame on those in charge of the U–2 program lest Khrushchev infer that the President of the United States had lost control over the governing process.[7]

The real problem that the Paris Summit Conference should have considered was Berlin and a German treaty, not Powers and the U–2. Khrushchev prevented such a discussion because he did not want a solution of the Berlin question except on his own terms, and that he could not have. When he went to East Berlin later in May, he avoided signing a peace treaty with the

[6] Sherman Adams, *Firsthand Report. The Story of the Eisenhower Administration*, 455–56.

[7] Eisenhower, *Waging the Peace*, 558.

East Germans because he had failed to split Western unity and did not dare risk denying Western access to Berlin.

Luckily for the United States, Khrushchev's brinkmanship in Paris failed to break the Western alliance, and his barroom tactics helped restore badly needed unity. Although the United States government appeared clumsy in the U–2 affair, Khrushchev succeeded in saving the battered prestige of American diplomacy by his antics in Paris.

The Paris Summit Conference revealed Soviet views of this diplomatic method. It was not the means to settle international problems because Khrushchev could have used the meeting for a talk over Russo-American relations and the Berlin question with the advantage on his side. Instead he chose to use the conference to further Soviet prestige by an ultimatum, threats, and obscenities. He harmed the summit conference as a serious method of dealing with the Soviet Union. Should a Soviet leader ever sincerely desire a summit conference, he may not be trusted by the Western powers because of Khrushchev's performance in Paris.

15

A Verdict

THE FRUITS of these summit conferences warrant their use to a limited degree as a regular procedure in diplomacy. But their record is proof that meetings of heads of governments alone will not solve the ills of the world.

At Paris in 1919 four men wrote a peace treaty which contributed to another war and helped establish the Nazi tyranny. The redeeming feature of the treaty was the League of Nations, but it should never have been in a peace treaty. The Herculean labors of Wilson brought on his collapse; the failure of the treaty harmed his reputation.

Although the Munich Conference saved the peace for one year, it destroyed Czechoslovak independence and ultimately helped bring the country under Communist control. The conference led Hitler to believe that Britain and France would put up only token opposition to his Polish coup. This conference was the result of the weakness of the Western nations before the rearmed might of Germany. If the balance of power had been different, the conference would have been different. In the long run, it saved the West because the agreement allowed Great Britain to complete her defenses for the Battle of Britain.

The Teheran Conference determined the future map of Europe when the decision was made for an Anglo-American invasion from the west and a Russian attack from the east. Of all the wartime conferences, this one has had the most lasting effect on the political outlines of Europe; its significance has been but dimly understood. The division of East and West which stemmed from this conference has lasted longer than the Treaty of Versailles. Certainly for the Western leaders, the results were unforeseen. Although this conference helped to achieve victory through co-ordination of plans, its final result has been far greater.

The influence of the Yalta Conference has been exaggerated, but little could be done once the Red Army occupied Central Europe. This occupation was a by-product of the Teheran Conference, a decision which on the surface was one of purely military substance. Yalta must be considered against the background of the period: Germany had not yet surrendered, the atomic bomb had not yet been detonated at Los Alamos, and Japan was still a strong foe. The meetings of the heads of government accomplished nothing that could not have been achieved through regular channels of negotiations if the West had been insistent enough. At Yalta much was glossed over, and basic differences were not honestly faced because Soviet armies were needed in the war. If the agreements had been seriously and conscientiously observed by Stalin, the Yalta Conference might have succeeded, but then Stalin would not have been Stalin and Soviet Russia an entirely different nation.

On paper, Potsdam was useful: German occupation was

arranged, the Nazi satellites were to be handled through conferences, and preparations were begun for the final peace treaties. The failure was owing to the same reasons which ruined Yalta: Soviet aims and Soviet power. However, the conference educated the United States, and particularly President Truman, in the ways of the Soviet Union. The results could have been worse if Churchill, Truman, and Attlee had not foiled Stalin's attempted thievery.

The Geneva Conference of 1955 revealed how little the East and West would risk upsetting the balance of power. Despite an avalanche of propaganda, nothing was changed, nor were serious negotiations even attempted.

No conference was so farcical as the abortive Paris Conference of 1960 when the United States and Soviet governments labored to look foolish. Yet the failure indicated the connection between a summit conference and the balance of power. Once again, Paris showed that it will be impossible to enter a conference room and by closing the door shut out the struggle for world power.

None of these summit conferences proved that the heads of government performed better, quicker, more accurately, or more efficiently than their foreign ministers or their professional diplomats. There is no proof that their presence made the agreement any better or any more durable; often the reverse was true. Although Wilson negotiated the Versailles Treaty, he could not convince the United States Senate to approve it. Chamberlain and Daladier had their parliaments approve the agreement, but they could never make Hitler observe it. Roosevelt, Churchill, and Truman obtained paper agreements from Stalin, but they could not enforce these without another world war. Despite his great wartime reputation, Eisenhower failed with Khrushchev and suffered great humiliation. Neither Eden, Macmillan, nor De Gaulle could help him.

These conferences failed to bridge the basic differences between the power blocs and sometimes even between democratic nations. Too often they served as vehicles for propaganda, gliding over the chasm of disagreement.

In hopes of reaching some compromise, in order to avoid a breakup, the leaders may side-step basic difficulties which should be resolutely faced, even though they are incapable of solution. The wartime meetings were filled with such instances, but because of the need for Soviet help the differences were deliberately glossed over.

Often it is useful in diplomacy to realize there is an honest difference and acknowledge it, but this is difficult, if not impossible in the summit conference. Because of the prestige involved, the heads of state may hesitate to bluntly confront each other with basic differences. These can be argued more easily on a lower level of the ambassador and the foreign minister.

Summit meetings do not make for greater international friendship simply because of drinks and dinners between heads of government. The reverse may be the case if one leader finds it advantageous to play off one opponent against another. Here Roosevelt was particularly vulnerable to Stalin's animosity towards Churchill. Neither do personal meetings always make for greater personal friendship and understanding. Wilson's talks with Clemenceau did not generate affection, and Hitler's meetings with Chamberlain produced only disgust.

Every summit meeting has been complicated by the need for time to prepare and to negotiate. Because heads of governments have limited time, it is difficult to prepare adequately for a meeting in which they will have to negotiate an intricate problem with someone whom they may never have met and do not understand. Once at the conference table the length of the meetings will be determined by problems back home where domestic issues need attention. Under pressure of time, someone in a summit conference may accept a dangerous solution to achieve agreement in order to return home to pressing domestic matters.

The timing of the summit conference can alter or change the outcome. The Yalta and Potsdam conferences were influenced by timing; after the defeat of Germany and Japan, the West could have been more brusque with Stalin, as indeed they were in the conference over the peace treaties. When the Munich Conference came, British armaments were only beginning to be improved and production increased; two or three years later Britain would possess adequate forces. An earlier meeting would have found the Germans less able to threaten the democracies. The Geneva meeting came too late to bring the Soviet leaders to agreement; a meeting in 1953 soon after Stalin's death might have produced a more solid agreement. The timing of the U–2 and the Paris meeting was incredibly bad.

Despite the speed of transportation and communications, the need to ponder the multitude of possibilities is more necessary than ever, and this would be difficult for a politician to accomplish, especially one who can devote two weeks at the most to decisions which mean life and death to millions. Negotiations ought to be attempted by someone who can devote full time to the task without keeping one ear cocked to domestic problems in Washington, London, or Paris.

At a summit conference a head of government engaged in negotiating an important agreement while operating within a time limit may make a poor decision in haste. Someone away from the conference who would not be so pressed for a speedy decision might see the error before approving the settlement.

Is it the prime role of a premier or a president to bargain and negotiate? Should this not be left to the professional diplomat who can be more easily sacrificed than the head of the government? By the use of stenographers, telegraph, radio, and telephone, the ambassador can keep his chief fully informed of the trend of the negotiations. If the negotiations are long and protracted, there will not be the rush because of time, and there will not be as great pressure to reach a hasty compromise in order to end the meeting.

Although the President of the United States is responsible for foreign policy, he is not required to personally negotiate every important agreement with other heads of government. Wilson's difficulties indicate the dangers for one mortal who attempted to negotiate a difficult treaty, make important foreign policy decisions, and govern the United States from Paris.

A remedy for the United States could be a statesman with long experience, good health, a vigorous mind, and without political ambitions. He could be appointed ambassador-at-large as the personal representative of the President with full negotiating powers. Modern communications would enable the President to maintain contact with his personal representative. Once the agreement was completed, the President could attend a summit conference for the purpose of signing the instrument and conferring with other heads of government.[1]

The summit conference is based on the assumption that only a head of government can negotiate the agreement and that he is the best available diplomat. Because a head of government has been successful in politics is no guarantee that he is fully qualified for an important summit conference. If a negotiation is desired, a nation will participate regardless of whether the negotiator is a president, premier, secretary of state, foreign minister, or ambassador.

In important negotiations the head of government should make the final decisions, but he ought not to be involved in the daily stresses of negotiating. He is needed to stand off and consider the negotiations and their place in the nation's general welfare. In war the commander-in-chief is not placed on the front line in order to assure victory but rather in the best position to direct the battle and the campaign.

Theoretically the process of negotiating at the summit ought to be quiet, cut off from the world without diverting influences, while statesmen quietly negotiate like medieval monks seeking heaven, but this has never occurred in the history of summit conferences. It is doubtful if this can be fully achieved in modern government. The Paris Conference in 1919 met under

[1] Dean Acheson, *Meetings at the Summit: A Study in the Diplomatic Method*, 25–26.

intense pressure to write a treaty because treaties were considered necessary to end war. The delegates were constantly harassed by the turmoil and problems that grew out of the postwar tumult. The Munich Conference met under the threat of war if there were no agreement satisfactory to Hitler. Teheran and Yalta conferences occurred with the burden of a world war always influencing the statesmen. The Potsdam conference was the longest of the three conferences during the war, but the desire of two new administrations interested in returning to domestic problems intensified the drive for speedy agreement. The Geneva meeting, with gigantic staffs and monster news conferences, wherein each side tried to score points, did not facilitate a quiet atmosphere conducive to thoughtful negotiation. In 1960 the Powers affair and Khrushchev's threats over Berlin doomed the negotiations.

The Churchill theory of the summit conference fails because of the stresses and problems of the political world which cannot be shut out by the conference-room door. It is gambling with peace to thrust the already overburdened heads of government into such a struggle. If sincere negotiations are desired, the burdens of those who negotiate ought to be lightened, not increased. Pressure of work can divert a president's attention, lead to confusion, and allow basic misunderstandings which could later bring a power confrontation and perhaps war.

No one can cut off power in a summit conference because the stand which heads of government take, their ideas, and viewpoints will reflect power and their willingness to use it. Achievements at the conference often succeed or fail through power. Power is not checked outside the conference-room door, and it is naïve to imagine that power can be taken out of international politics. None of the conferences ever met in a power vacuum, and none will ever do so, for what is the national state but the embodiment of the power of millions of people? It is this confrontation of power in the heads of governments which has made the summit conference dangerous.

The Yalta and Potsdam agreements were stillborn because the British and Americans either lacked the power or were unable to exert it. Stalin's armies held much of Central Europe, and they could not be pushed out except by the use of force in another world war. Stalin lost at Potsdam wherever he could not exert the power of the Russian armies. Chamberlain and Daladier were helpless at Munich because of the weakness of Anglo-French armed forces. If Wilson and Roosevelt had been more certain that Congress would back them with the necessary power, they could have given Europe a more forceful lead. Khrushchev secured nothing at Geneva in 1955 because of the power stalemate; he could only have the U–2 flights cancelled at Paris. Yet because of Western power he did not dare go any further in settling the Berlin question unilaterally.

Personality and training of the heads of government are powerful influences in the meetings. To date, none has been adequately trained, and few have had the personality for the task. Roosevelt was basically insular, almost isolationist in some of his beliefs, he played too much by ear, depending on his own interpretations. His ignorance of Russian affairs was apparent in his belief that if he could overcome Stalin's suspicions and keep the British from being so imperial, Soviet foreign policies would be altered. His charm which had been so successful with the American voters was not sufficient to overcome Russian ambitions.

Churchill saw many of the dangers in the problems discussed at the summit conferences, but he was untrained as a diplomat. He lacked the subtlety to evade Stalin's thrusts and to combat his guile. He was always too eager to talk and debate.

Stalin was a shrewd, suspicious peasant, prepared to seize whatever would benefit the Soviet Union. The gospels according to Marx, Engels, and Lenin never troubled him at the conference table. As a negotiator, he was calm, unhurried, and reserved. He did not wander off the topic, lecture the others, shout, nor rant. Where Soviet interests were at stake, he could be ruthless and, if need be, brutal. He must be ranked as one of the best amateur negotiators.[2]

Hitler did not negotiate at Munich and never really intended to do so. He desired only to crush his opponents through a victory that would enhance his power. Like Stalin, his chief accomplishments were owing to military strength and his opponents' weaknesses and irresolution.

Eisenhower had a brilliant record as a general who had harnessed a team to win a great victory when the team members were agreed on the goal. He could not win over Khrushchev who was not seeking the same goal.

Woodrow Wilson's personality often grated on those who had to negotiate with him. Of his sincerity there could be no doubt, but he had a regrettable tendency to pontificate.

Clemenceau was too engrossed with the immediate problem of French security to consider how his successors would deal with Germany. With the brilliant collection of French diplomats then available, there was no need for Clemenceau to be present at the conference.

Lloyd George labored hard to find a solution, and because he often sought any agreement, he seemed insincere. Yet he was ever the ambitious politician, thinking of the voters. He sought changes at the last moment in the treaty because of domestic political pressures.

Chamberlain let himself become involved in a summit conference with very inadequate preparation. Czechoslovakia was weakened badly in the fall of 1938 after the conference because of his shortsightedness and inadequate information. He had been a great believer in the need to let the heads of government negotiate instead of the professional diplomats. His experience as a Birmingham businessman had not fully toughened him to the

---

[2] Concerning Stalin as a negotiator, Anthony Eden wrote: "Marshal Stalin as a negotiator was the toughest proposition of all. Indeed, after something like thirty years' experience of international conferences of one kind and another, if I had to pick a team for going into a conference room, Stalin would be my first choice." (*The Reckoning*, 595).

rigors of negotiating with Hitler and Mussolini. His colleague Daladier was intelligent but badly frightened; he should have stayed in Paris.

Khrushchev saw conferences as a device for propaganda, not for serious negotiating. He used the Geneva Conference to find out how far the Western powers would let him go in Central Europe, and his diagnosis paid off when he destroyed Hungary in 1956. His Paris performance left Western statesmen afraid of another summit conference with him.

Reputations have been destroyed or harmed by these conferences. Wilson was condemned for being hoodwinked by Clemenceau and Lloyd George into accepting terms that brought a new world war. Chamberlain bore the burden of the Munich Conference to his grave. Roosevelt has been denounced for supposed giveaways to the Russians in secret deals at Teheran and Yalta. Churchill has been damned by the Poles in exile for his actions regarding Poland. Eisenhower ended his term in office with the failure of the Paris Conference. No other act of Hitler's so revealed his true character to the world as his destruction of the Munich Agreement in March, 1939. The political career of Edouard Daladier never recovered from the destruction of the Munich Agreement by Hitler. Orlando was never again to be prime minister because his opponents stopped him with his record at Paris.

Yet it is unfair to accuse politicians who meet at summit conferences if they cannot foresee the future. They are neither prophets nor philosopher kings, but only imperfect men, the sum of their past experiences, training, and human weaknesses. Omniscience cannot suddenly be expected from these men when they go to summit conferences.

Rival leaders in a summit conference meet as prima donnas, accustomed to exerting their influence over party members and lesser politicians. At home their slightest utterance is too often worth large headlines in the daily press, but at the summit conference they are dealing with their peers who do not have to

accept their ideas and statements because they come from another prime minister or a president. There can be an exaggerated
pride of a Roosevelt who imagined that by force of personality
he could charm Stalin into a drastic change in policy.

Presidents and premiers from differing political systems,
speaking different languages, and with limited experience in
negotiating may find communicating their ideas to the other
heads of government difficult in a summit conference. Certainly
Hitler and Chamberlain left Munich without really understanding each other. Despite two meetings with Stalin, Roosevelt does
not seem to have understood the Soviet leader much better nor
to have received any fresh insights into Russian policy. Did
Stalin fully understand Roosevelt and Churchill? Could he have
assumed that they expected him to exercise full political control
wherever he had military domination? He could have thought
they were raising objections for the record and would not be so
naïve as to imagine that he would ever permit capitalist political parties in his empire.

When the heads of government approach a summit conference, they bring with them their own prejudices, biases, myths,
and fears. These are not checked at the conference door enabling
the leaders to become open-minded judges. Wilson went to Paris
determined to set the Old World right and save it from its sinful
ways. Roosevelt feared the sneaky British. Clemenceau went to
the peace conference resolved to weaken Germany forever. Certainly Stalin could not shrug off a lifetime's suspicions of the
Western democracies.

At the summit conference the heads of government are not
as free to negotiate as they imagine. Forces which they cannot
control may exert a powerful influence: public opinion, history,
the actions of other nations. The American popular feeling that
Roosevelt arranged a secret deal at Yalta and Potsdam limited
Eisenhower's negotiating at Geneva. Churchill's freedom of
action was curtailed by Britain's military weakness and her need
of help from the two stronger allies. Certainly Roosevelt would

have acted differently if there had been no need to win a world war. At the Paris Summit Conference of 1960, four statesmen could not negotiate because of one U–2 plane that had been shot out of the sky.

Summit diplomacy is a difficult process for the President of the United States because any agreement which even smells like a treaty must have Senate approval. Thus whenever a president journeys to a summit conference, he is restricted in his freedom of action. He can take senators from the opposing political party with him to insure passage of any treaty, but in a summit conference, the presence of senators would dilute presidential authority.

In a summit conference the health of the negotiators becomes a significant factor. Could someone suffering from a heart condition withstand the labors of a prolonged summit conference or one hastily called in a dangerous crisis? An upset stomach could leave a president in a poor state to negotiate. If an illness should suddenly strike, will it be considered a diplomatic affliction by others? Dare the statesmen risk postponement after there has been so much preconference publicity? If a professional diplomat becomes ill, he can be easily replaced. Who can replace a president in a summit conference? Colonel Edward House was a poor replacement for Wilson during his illness at the Paris Conference of 1919.

In the postwar summit meetings too little attention has been paid to purpose and content; the conferences tended to become charades that would save the world. The feeling that the Cold War was merely the result of misunderstanding and that if Eisenhower could only charm Khrushchev all would be well was as erroneous as some of Roosevelt's views regarding Stalin. If such profound problems could be solved so easily by personality alone, why waste a president on such a task? Are there not others who would succeed better as the charmers? This formula failed because it did not solve the basic difficulty of the cause of the Cold War. After the meetings at Geneva, the fundamental problem was unresolved because it could not be solved by the heads of government in a few days meeting. The belief that charm alone could save the day served only to confuse the democracies whose peoples tended to believe, with their leaders, that meetings between statesmen would alter problems based on power relationships.

Before launching into future summit conferences, these questions should be asked: "Is this trip necessary? Will this conference accomplish anything serious?" No summit conference should be undertaken without serious consideration of all the consequences. Would a face-to-face meeting really alter the situation? Roosevelt believed that he could somehow inveigle the Soviet dictator into changing his outlook, too long colored by the nefarious British. Chamberlain was eager to push aside the professional diplomats and personally negotiate with European rulers. Eisenhower took a long heralded trip to Geneva which changed nothing. Only the trip to Potsdam changed anything: Harry Truman's attitude.

If there are future summit conferences with an agreement as the goal, careful preparation and planning are imperative. Wilson's failure to plan adequately for the conference was a major factor in the confusion and delay which characterized the peace conference for so many weeks. Chamberlain went off to Munich without any joint planning with the French and with only a minimum of advice from his own staffs. The failure to have joint planning before their summit conferences with Stalin, handicapped Churchill, Roosevelt, and Truman.

Yet if there is a vast amount of preconference planning with the necessary cramming of ideas and facts into the chief delegate's head, great expectations will be aroused among the public. As the flurry of preparation for a conference increases, the public will more certainly expect concrete results. When there is no solution, greater will be the disappointment.

In the future, calling a summit conference amid a world crisis should be undertaken only as a last, desperate resort. The

U–2 affair cast such a cloud over the Russo-American relations that any meeting under such conditions was foolhardy. The Munich Conference was a bad solution to a complicated problem which had lasted hundreds of years and which Anglo-French leaders did not fully understand. To meet under threat of war was not auspicious for a just solution, yet the British were particularly driven toward the meeting by the belief that high-level meetings in 1914 might have made clear the British determination to enter the conflict on the side of France and thus the war could have been avoided.

Whether a meeting of the heads of government in 1914 or 1939 could have stopped hostilities is doubtful. A conference attended by Kaiser Wilhelm II, Czar Nicholas II, Kaiser Franz Josef, President Raymond Poincaré, and Herbert Asquith in the summer of 1914 would have been interesting, but could this quintet have prevented war? When these men realized the danger of conflict, it was too late, for they either would not or could not halt the rush to war.

A second summit meeting was suggested in September, 1939, but all parties would not agree on the concessions to be made before the conference convened. Hitler would not withdraw from Poland, and the British and French would not join in the meeting unless he did. By starting the hostilities, Hitler made a summit conference impossible. After the Munich Conference and the German seizure of Czechoslovakia in 1939, the British government feared a summit conference because of domestic political repercussions. In such a meeting, Hitler would have had advantages: His armies had won swift victories, and the Soviet Union had become his ally.

The summit conference does present an opportunity for making proposals and counter proposals within a short period of time. There is no need for the usual time lapse while the proposals are referred to higher echelons of government. Those who will make the final decisions are there negotiating and can make the decisions at the conference. This was one of the chief arguments for summit conferences with Stalin and Khrushchev. Except for the wartime conferences when important military and strategic decisions were made, little has come from summit conferences with the Soviet leaders that fostered better East-West relations.

Another argument favoring the summit conference relates to the power of making decisions that involve different areas of government. A diplomat is not usually entrusted with such authority but only the head of government. Only on a high level can decisions be made swiftly which involve diverse fields of government.

Significant agreements have been negotiated without the presence of the heads of government. They were not needed at the conference in San Francisco in 1945 when the United Nations Charter was drafted. The United States completed a peace treaty with Japan in 1951 without the President, the emperor, or prime ministers. The heads of government were absent from the negotiations over the North Atlantic Treaty and the Treaty of Rome establishing the European Economic Community.

The Test Ban Treaty was achieved in 1963 without a summit conference. Such a treaty could scarcely have been negotiated by the heads of government because of their lack of experience and shortness of time. The treaty was no worse and probably much better because the heads of government were absent. If the treaty had been negotiated by the leaders in a summit conference, the Kennedy administration would have been forced to defend not only the treaty but also the President's negotiations. By avoiding a summit conference, more attention could be focused on the virtues and defects in the Test Ban Treaty. Nor would the Test Ban Treaty have been achieved if the negotiations had been attempted by the summit conference of eighteen heads of government which the Soviet government recommended to the United Nations on September 19, 1963.

Instead of a formal summit conference, if the heads of government want to meet, let them have face-to-face, personal conferences. Such personal diplomacy between heads of government is ancient and honorable; it will certainly continue, but the meetings should be for purposes of discussion without formal, written agreement. From such meetings something could be learned of the personality and attitudes of the other leader. If such meetings are to be continued, the more regular the procedure the better, for the meetings will have less dramatic appeal and the public will not expect as much from them. Yet even these meetings have their dangers. The Kennedy-Khrushchev meeting in 1961 after the Bay of Pigs fiasco did not prevent Khrushchev from misjudging Kennedy's reactions to the introduction of Soviet rockets into Cuba.

The formal summit conference could serve as the occasion for the signing of a final agreement, not the negotiation which should have been pursued by the professionals. The formal summit conference of three or more heads of government to negotiate an agreement is a very dangerous remedy. Only in case of absolute necessity should it be prescribed.

Summit conference ought not to be used as an antibiotic, believing that frequent doses will cure the patient. The summit conference can never be a quick cheap cure for international ills whose treatment requires time, labor, and thought. Quiet diplomacy without publicity, presidents, and prime ministers is still imperative.

Bibliography

I. Primary Sources

A. *Newspapers and Periodicals*

Current Digest of the Soviet Press.
Department of State Bulletin.
Economist.
London *Times.*
New York Times.
Time.

B. *Printed Collected Documents*

American Foreign Policy. Current Documents. 1958. Washington, D.C., 1962.
United States Senate, Committee on Foreign Relations. *Events*

Incident to the Summit Conference, Hearings, 86 Cong. 2 sess. May 27–June 2, 1960, Washington, D.C., 1960.

Department of State. *Background of Heads of Government Conference, 1960.* Washington, D.C., 1960.

———. *The Geneva Conference of Heads of Government, July 18–23, 1955.* Washington, D.C., 1955.

———. *The Geneva Meeting of Foreign Ministers, October 27–November 16, 1955.* Washington D.C., 1955.

Documents and Materials Relating to the Eve of the Second World War. 2 vols. New York, 1948–49.

Documents on British Foreign Policy. Third Series. Vol. II. Edited by E. L. Woodward and Rohan Butler. London, 1949.

Documents on German Foreign Policy, 1918–1945. Series C, Vol. I; D, Vols. I, II, VII. Washington, D.C., 1949.

Foreign Relations of the United States. Diplomatic Papers, 1942. Vol. III, Washington, D.C., 1961.

Diplomatic Papers. The Conference of Berlin (The Potsdam Conference), 1945. 2 vols. Washington, D.C., 1960.

Diplomatic Papers. The Conference at Cairo and Teheran, 1943. Washington, D.C., 1961.

Diplomatic Papers. The Conference at Malta and Yalta, 1945. Washington, D.C., 1955.

Diplomatic Papers. The Soviet Union, 1933–1939. Washington, D.C., 1952.

The Lansing Papers, 1914–1920. 2 vols. Washington, D.C., 1939.

Paris Peace Conference, 1919. Vols. III–VI. Washington, D.C., 1946.

Nazi Conspiracy and Aggression. 8 vols. Supplements. Washington, D.C., 1946.

Parliamentary Debates. House of Commons.

Stalin's Correspondence with Churchill, Atlee, Roosevelt and Truman, 1941–1945. London, 1958.

"Teheran Conference: Unpublished Soviet Documents," *International Affairs* (Moscow) Vols. 7, 8 (July, August, 1961), 133–45, 110–22.

The Trials of the Major War Criminals Before the International *Military Tribunal, Proceedings and Documents.* 42 vols. Nürnberg, 1947–49.

C. *Printed Memoirs, Diaries, Speeches*

Adams, Sherman. *Firsthand Report. The Story of the Eisen-hower Administration.* New York, 1961.

Bryant, Arthur. *Triumph in the West. A History of the War Years Based on the Diaries of Field-Marshal Lord Alanbrooke, Chief of the Imperial General Staff.* New York, 1959.

Byrnes, James. *All in One Lifetime.* New York, 1958.

——. *Speaking Frankly.* New York, 1947.

Churchill, Winston S. *Closing the Ring.* Boston, 1951.

——. *The Hinge of Fate.* Boston, 1950.

——. *Triumph and Tragedy.* Boston, 1953.

Eden, Anthony. *Full Circle.* Boston, 1960.

——. *The Reckoning.* Boston, 1965.

Eisenhower, Dwight D., *The White House Years. Mandate for Change, 1953–1956.* New York, 1963.

——. *The White House Years. Waging Peace, 1956–1961.* New York, 1965.

House, Edward M. *The Intimate Papers of Colonel House.* Vol. IV. Boston, 1928.

Kleist, Peter. *Zwischen Hitler und Stalin.* Berlin, 1950.

Lansing, Robert. *The Big Four and Others of the Peace Con-ference.* Boston, 1921.

Leahy, William D. *I Was There. The Personal Story of the Chief of Staff to Presidents Roosevelt and Truman Based on his Notes and Diaries Made at the Time.* New York, 1950.

Leonhard, Wolfgang. *Child of the Revolution.* London, 1957.

Mantoux, Paul. *Les délibérations du conseil des quatre (24 mars–28 juin 1919).* 2 vols. Paris, 1955.

Perkins, Francis. *The Roosevelt I Knew.* New York, 1946.

Roosevelt, Elliott. *As He Saw It.* New York, 1946.

Stimson, Henry L., and Bundy, McGeorge. *On Active Service in Peace and War*. New York, 1948.

Truman, Harry S. *Year of Decisions*. Garden City, 1955.

What Really Happened at Paris: The Story of the Peace Conference 1918–1919 by American Delegates. Ed. by Edward M. House and Charles Seymour. New York, 1921.

II. *Secondary Sources*

Acheson, Dean. *Meetings at the Summit: A Study in the Diplomatic Method*. Durham, 1958.

Alsop, Joseph and Stewart. *The Reporter's Trade*. New York, 1958.

Baker, Ray Stannard. *Woodrow Wilson: Life and Letters*. Vol. VIII. New York, 1939.

———. *Woodrow Wilson and World Settlement; Written from his Unpublished and Personal Material*. 3 vols. New York, 1923.

Barraclough, G. *Survey of International Affairs, 1956–1958*. London, 1962.

———, and Rachel F. Wall. *Survey of International Affairs, 1955–1956*. London, 1960.

Bell, Carol. *Negotiations from Strength*. New York, 1963.

Berding, Andrew. *Foreign Affairs and You! How American Foreign Policy is Made and What it Means to You*. New York, 1962.

Bostick, Darwin, "The German-Polish Boundary at the Paris Peace Conference" (unpublished M.A. thesis, North Texas State University, 1963).

Brown, Dora M. "Woodrow Wilson in the Council of Four: A Re-evaluation" (unpublished M.A. thesis, North Texas State University, 1965).

Donovan, Robert J. *Eisenhower: The Inside Story*. New York, 1956.

Dulles, Allan. *The Craft of Intelligence*. New York, 1963.

Ehrman, John. *Grand Strategy.* Vol. V. London, 1956.

Emerson, William R. "F.D.R.," *The Ultimate Decision: The President as Commander-in-Chief.* New York, 1960.

Eubank, Keith. "The British Pledge to Poland: Prelude to War," *Southwestern Social Science Quarterly,* Vol. XLV (March, 1965), 340–48.

———. *Munich.* Norman, 1963.

Feis, Herbert. *Between War and Peace. The Potsdam Conference.* Princeton, 1960.

———, *Churchill, Roosevelt, Stalin. The War They Waged and the Peace They Sought.* Princeton, 1957.

———. *Japan Subdued. The Atomic Bomb and the End of the War in the Pacific.* Princeton, 1961.

Field, Henry, "How FDR did his Homework," *Saturday Review of Literature,* Vol. XLVI (July 8, 1961), 8–10.

Gramont, Sanche, de. *The Secret War. The Story of International Espionage since World War II.* New York, 1962.

Gunther, John. *Roosevelt in Retrospect. A Profile in History.* New York, 1950.

Hankey, Maurice. *Diplomacy by Conference. Studies in Public Affairs 1920–1946.* New York, 1946.

———. *The Supreme Control at the Paris Peace Conference. 1919.* London, 1963.

Hoover, Herbert. *The Ordeal of Woodrow Wilson.* New York, 1958.

Hughes, Emmet John. *The Ordeal of Power.* New York, 1963.

Inklé, Fred Charles. *How Nations Negotiate.* New York, 1964.

Kirkpatrick, Ivone. *Mussolini. A Study in Power.* New York, 1946.

Kissinger, Henry A. *The Necessity for Choice. Prospects of American Foreign Policy.* New York, 1961.

Lederer, Ivo J. *Yugoslavia at the Paris Peace Conference.* New Haven, 1963.

Leonhard, Wolfgang. *The Kremlin Since Stalin.* New York, 1962.

Matloff, Maurice. *United States Army in World War II. The War*

Department. Strategic Planning for Coalition Warfare 1943–1944. Washington, D.C., 1959.

Mosely, Philip E. *The Kremlin and World Politics. Studies in Soviet Policy and Action.* New York, 1960.

Nelson, Harold I. *Land and Power. British and Allied Policy on Germany's Frontiers. 1916–19.* London, 1963.

Postan, M. M. *British War Production.* London, 1952.

Ripka, Hubert. *Munich: Before and After.* London, 1939.

Roetter, Charles. *The Diplomatic Art. An Informal History of World Diplomacy.* Philadelphia, 1962.

Rostow, W. W. *The United States in the World Arena.* New York, 1960.

Rovere, Richard E. *Affairs of State. The Eisenhower Years.* New York, 1958.

Sherwood, Robert E. *Roosevelt and Hopkins. An Intimate History.* New York, 1948.

Shirer, William L. *Rise and Fall of the Third Reich: A History of Nazi Germany.* New York, 1960.

Snell, John. *Illusion and Necessity. The Diplomacy of Global War, 1939–45.* Boston, 1963.

———, et al. *The Meaning of Yalta.* Baton Rouge, 1956.

Speier, Hans. *Divided Berlin. The Anatomy of Soviet Political Blackmail.* New York, 1961.

Stettinius, Edward R., Jr., *Roosevelt and the Russians. The Yalta Conference.* Ed. by Walter Johnson. Garden City, 1949.

Taylor, A. J. P. *The Origins of the Second World War.* London, 1961.

Tillman, Seth P. *Anglo-American Relations at the Paris Peace Conference of 1919.* Princeton, 1961.

Walworth, Arthur. *Woodrow Wilson.* 2 vols. New York, 1958.

Wighton, Charles. *Adenauer. A Critical Biography.* New York, 1958.

Windsor, Philip. *City on Leave. A History of Berlin, 1945–1962.* New York, 1963.

Wise, David and Thomas B. Ross. *The U–2 Affair.* New York, 1962.

Woodward, Llewellyn. *British Foreign Policy in the Second World War.* London, 1962.

Index

A

Adenauer, Konrad: 156–57, 163, 171
Aga Khan: 25
Alamogordo, New Mexico: 127
Alexander I, Czar: 7
Alexander, Field Marshal Harold: 82
Andaman Islands: 56
Anglo-American guarantee (1919):
  17–19
Anglo-French ultimatum (1938): 37
Antonov, General A. I.: 83
Appeasement: 39–40, 45, 49
Article 231 (Versailles Treaty): 25–
  26, 32
Asquith, Herbert: 207
Atlantic Charter: 52

Atlee, Clement: 128–29, 196
Atomic bomb: 81, 127; Test Ban
  Treaty, 208
Austria: *Anschluss,* 34; peace treaty,
  131, 138, 140; discussed in Potsdam
  Conference, 120

B

Baker, Ray Stannard: 13
Baku, U.S.S.R.: 173–74
Balfour, Lord: 9
Balkans: Churchill on, 60, 65
Baltic Sea: Roosevelt on, 62, 69
Baltic States: Roosevelt and Stalin on,
  72
Baroduc, Pierre: 153

Bay of Pigs: 209

Beneš, Eduard: 34–35, 39; and Munich Agreement, 46

Berchtesgaden, Germany: 37

Berlin, German: 27; blockade of, 135–36; Khrushchev on occupation of, 168, 173–74, 192–93

Bermuda: 138

Bessarabia, U.S.S.R.: 51

Bevin, Ernest: 128–29

Bierut, Boleslaw: 92

Bismarck, Otto von: 7

Bliss, General Tasker H.: 27

Bohlen, Charles: 82

Bonnet, Georges: 37–38

Brooke, General Alan: 64, 70

Bulganin, Nikolai: 141; at Geneva Conference, 146–52; and "open-skies" proposal, 150–51, 155; projected new image, 153–54; and "Spirit of Geneva," 157–58; correspondence with Eisenhower, 161–63

Bulgaria: 75, 81, 119, 123–34, 126–27, 131, 134

Burma: 56

Byrnes, James F.: 131

C

Cairo Conference: 56–57

Camp David talks: 170

Catherine the Great: 46

Cavallero, General Ugo: 27

Central Intelligence Agency: 4, 175–76, 188–89, 191–92

Chamberlain, Neville: 197; on Czechoslovakia, 35; sends Runciman to Prague, 36; at Berchtesgaden meeting, 36–37; appeasement policy, 38–40, 48, 140; failure to confer with Daladier, 40, 43–44; at Munich Conference, 41–44, 49; confers with Mastny and Masařík, 45–46; agreement with Hitler, 46; helplessness at Munich, 201; as negotiator 202–203;

reputation, 203; understanding of Hitler, 204; failure to plan, 206

Chiang Kai-Shek: 56–57, 90–91, 99

China: 113; German concessions in, 23; Roosevelt on, 64; discussed at Potsdam Conference, 115–16; Eisenhower on, 147; see also Communist China

Churchill, Prime Minister Winston: 57, 158, 196–97; on summit conference, 5; career, 51–52; negotiating site for summit conference, 52–55; at Cairo Conference, 56–57; lack of accord with Roosevelt, 57; at Teheran Conference, 59–75; taunted by Stalin, 67, 70, 78; teased by Roosevelt, 76–77; negotiations over Yalta Conference, 80–81; private meeting with Stalin, 82; at Yalta Conference, 83–101; on Poland, 106–107; asks Truman for summit conference, 108–109; fears for Europe, 109; conference with Davies, 109–10; on Potsdam Conference, 112; private meeting with Truman, 113; at Potsdam Conference, 114–28; electoral defeat, 128–29; baited by Stalin, 130; on postwar summit conference, 136–38; training of, 201; reputation of, 203; action curtailed, 204; failure to plan, 206

Clark Kerr, Archibald: 89, 91, 106, 112–13

Clemenceau, Georges: 10, 12–13, 197; career, 14; in Council of Four, 16–30; as negotiator, 202

Cold War: 135–36, 145–46, 181, 205–206

Collective security treaty: proposed at Geneva Conference, 148–49

Colonies: 123

Communist China: 167–68, 174; and Paris Summit Conference, 189–90

Council of Foreign Ministers: 116, 118–19

Council of Ten: 11

Council of Four: origin of, 11–12; organization of, 12–14, 23–24, 30; personalities of members, 14–16; meetings, 16–29; lack of planning for, 29–30; significance of, 194

Crabbe, Commander Lionel: 192

Cunningham, Admiral Sir Andrew: 83

"Curzon line": 73–75, 87, 89, 91, 98

Czechoslovakia: 33ff., 81

D

Dairen, Manchuria: 69, 90, 99

Daladier, Edouard: 35–37, 40; failure to confer with Chamberlain, 40, 43–44; at Munich Conference, 41–45, 47, 49; confers with Czech diplomats, 45–46; helplessness at Munich, 201; as negotiator, 203

Dalmatia: 20–22

Danzig, Poland: 19–20

Dardanelles, Straits of: 69, 98, 123–24, 127, 133

Davies, Joseph W.: 109–10

Davis, Norman: 25

De Gaulle, Charles: 101, 167; at Paris Summit Conference, 3, 183–88; Stalin on, 59, 61, 83, 92; and postponement of summit conference, 170–71; and Khrushchev, 172; 181–82

De Jean, Maurice: 165

Dillon, Douglas: 173

Disarmament: 145, 149–50

Disraeli, Benjamin: 7

Dulles, Allan: 191

Dulles, John Foster: 138–39, 141; on Geneva Conference, 142, 158; on summit conference, 162–65; death of, 170; on U–2 flights, 177

E

Eden, Anthony: 67, 73, 82, 94, 96–97, 99, 120, 131; on summit conference, 139; at Geneva Conference, 142, 144–52; on Stalin, 201 n.

Egypt: 95

Eisenhower, President Dwight D.: 136, 141; at Paris Summit Conference, 3, 183–88; on summit conference, 137ff.; speech, July 15, 1955, 141–42; on Geneva Conference, 142; plans for Geneva Conference, 143; at Geneva Conference, 144–52; "open-skies" proposal, 150–51, 155; private talks, 153; tactics at Geneva Conference, 154–55; on results of Geneva Conference, 157; correspondence with Bulganin, 161–63; and United Nations summit conference, 167; and Macmillan, 169; and Khrushchev visit to United States, 170; and Adenauer, 171; and U–2 flights, 176, 179–80, 192; studies Khrushchev memorandum, 181–82; as negotiator, 202; reputation of, 203; influenced by Yalta Conference, 204; role in conferences, 205

Espionage: 190–92

Estonia: 51

F

Far East: Stalin on, 69; Roosevelt-Stalin conversation at Yalta, 90–91; Yalta tripartite agreement, 99–100, 104–105

Faure, Edgar: 139, 142; at Geneva Conference, 144–52

Finland: 51, 97, 119, 126–27, 131; Stalin on, 71

Fiume: 20–22

Foch, Marshal Ferdinand: 10, 27–28

Foreign Ministers' meeting: 169

Formosa: 69

France: military weakness of, 35; 47–48; Roosevelt on, 59, 101; Stalin on, 60–61; in Teheran agreement, 75; and zone of occupation in Germany, 84–85, 96–97; and summit conference, 137; and tripartite note, May 10, 1955, 139–40; and agreement, March 31, 1958, 165

Franco, General Francisco: 117

Franz Josef, Emperor: 33, 207

Frederick the Great: 46

G

Gates, Thomas: 182

Geneva Summit Conference: invitation to, 139–40; organization and planning, 140–41; Western disunity, 142–43, 154–55; size, 144; meetings, 144–52; foreign ministers' directive, 152; and press, 153; effects, 155–56; procedure, 156–57; results of, 157–59; significance of, 196; timing of, 198; and quiet diplomacy, 200

George, Walter F.: 139

German-Polish Nonaggression Pact, (1934): 101

Germany: in Council of Four, 16–17, 27–28; foreign ministry and Munich Conference, 42; discussed at Teheran, 61–62, 64–65, 67, 74, 77–78; discussed at Yalta, 84–86, 95, 97–98, 100; discussed at Potsdam, 116–17, 121–22, 128–30; in Cold War, 135–36; unification of, 145ff., 157; Khrushchev on, 168; see also West Germany

Gibraltar: 68

Godesberg, Germany: 37–38

Graham, Billy: 143

Great Britain: armed forces, 35, 47–48; elections, 100; foreign office on summit conference, 137; and tripartite note, May 10, 1955, 139–40; March 31, 1958, agreement, 165

Greece: 133–34; Stalin on, 93

Gromyko, Andrei: 80, 165, 181, 183

H

Hacha, Emil: 45

Hagerty, James: 153

Hankey, Maurice: 13

Harriman, Averell: 54, 80, 90–91, 106, 112–13

Henderson, Neville: 36

Henlein, Konrad: 34–36

Herter, Christian: and Senate Foreign Relations Committee, 171; speech, April 4, 1960, 172–73; and U–2 flights, 179

Hitler, Adolf: 110, and Czechoslovakia, 33, 48; at November 5, 1937, conference, 34; and Henlein, 34; signs May 30 directive, 36; speech at Nürnberg, November 13, 1938, 36; at Berchtesgaden Conference, 37; at Godesberg Conference, 37–38; and war over Czechoslovakia, 38; invitation to Munich Conference, 39–40; at Munich Conference, 41–45; agreement with Chamberlain, 46; and effects of Munich Conference, 47; negotiations with Stalin, 50–51, 55; Stalin on 61–62; Roosevelt on, 62; as negotiator, 202; character of, 203; and Chamberlain, 204; and summit conference in 1939, 207

Hodža, Milan: 36

Hopkins, Harry: 53, 57, 66, 71, 80, 97; meetings with Stalin, 110–11

House, Colonel Edward: 10, 17

Hungary: 81, 97, 119, 126–27, 131, 134

I

Ilyichev, Leonid: 153

India: Roosevelt on, 59

Indochina: Roosevelt on, 59, 91

Inland waterways: Truman proposal concerning, 124

Iran: 75, 89, 125, 133–34

Italy: claims discussed in Council of Four, 20–22; discussed at Teheran, 69, 73; and peace treaty, 131; discussed at Potsdam, 119, 121, 126–27, 129

J

Japan: 134; and German concessions in China, 23; discussed at Cairo Conference, 56–57; Russian assurances regarding, 60, 99; Stalin's demands concerning, 90; and peace treaty, 208

Joseph II, Emperor (Holy Roman Empire): 33

K

Kennedy, President John F.: 208–209

Khrushchev, Nikita S.: 162, 165; at Paris Summit Conference, 3–4, 183–88; speech, July 4, 1955, 141; at Geneva Conference, 146–52; ignored by Eisenhower, 153; new image of, 153–54; and "open-skies" proposal, 151, 155; affected by Geneva Conference, 155–56; rise to power, 160–61; conception of summit conference, 161; speech, November 6, 1957, 161; Minsk speech, January 22, 1958, 163; torpedoes summit conference, June 1958, 165–66; on United States intervention in Lebanon and Syria, 166–67; and summit conference in Security Council, 167–68; demands end of Berlin occupation, 168; February 24, 1959 speech, 168; withdraws ultimatum over Berlin, 169; visit to United States, 170; and De Gaulle, 171–72; Baku speech, April 25, 1960, 173–74; and U-2 flights, 177–80; talk with De Gaulle, May 15, 1960, 181–82; at Paris Summit Conference, 188–90; and Germany, 192–93; as negotiator, 203; and Kennedy, 209

King, Admiral Ernest J.: 104

Knowland, William A.: 137

Kolchak, Admiral A. V.: 24

Königsberg (Kalininigrad), U.S.S.R.: 124–25

Korea: 69, 91, 136

Kozlov, Frol: 157

Kudryavtsev, Sergei M.: 187

Kuril Islands: 90, 99

L

Lansing, Robert: 10

Latvia: 51

League of Nations: 18, 63

Leahy, Admiral William D.: 57

Lebanon: 133, 166

Libya: 133

Lloyd George, David: 9–10; complaints about publicity, 11, 13; career, 14–15; in Council of Four, 16–30; as negotiator, 202

London, Treaty of: 21–22

M

MacArthur, General Douglas: 104

McCarthy, Senator Joseph: 138, 141

Macmillan, Harold: at Paris Summit Conference, 3, 183–88; advocates summit conference, 169; and Adenauer, 171; and Khrushchev memorandum, May 15, 1960, 181–82

Maginot Line: 35, 48

Maisky, Ivan: 85

Malinovsky, Marshal Rodion I: 181, 183

Malta: 81

Manchuria: 69

Mantoux, Paul: 13

Maria Theresa, Empress: 33

Marshal, General George C.: 64, 83

Marshal Plan: 135

Masařík, Hubert: 45–46

Mastny, Vojtéch: 45–46

Matsu: 139

Mediterranean theater of war: Churchill on, 60, 65

Mendès-France, Pierre: 138

Metternich, Alexander Klemens von: 7

Mikoyan, Anastas: 157

Molotov, V. M.: 64, 73, 82, 88, 91, 106, 112–13, 123, 126–27, 131, 140

Montreux Convention: 69, 98, 123–24, 133

Munich Agreement: 44, 101

Munich Conference: 158, 169, 173; meetings, 41–44; lack of planning for, 44; effects of, 47–49; significance of, 49, 194–95, 207; and quiet diplomacy, 200

Murmansk, U.S.S.R.: 51

Murphy, Robert: 170

Musolini, Benito: 38–40; at Munich Conference, 41–45

N

National Aeronautics Space Administration: 178

Nazi-Soviet Nonaggression Pact: 50–51, 73

Nehru, Jawaharlal: 167

Nicholas I, Czar: 77

Nicholas II, Czar: 207

Nixon, Vice-President Richard M.: 157–58, 177

North Atlantic Treaty Organization (NATO): 136, 138, 146ff., 157, 208

Norway: 177

Nürnberg, Germany: 36, 48

O

Oder-Neisse line: 62, 72, 89, 90–91, 121–22, 130

"Open-skies" proposal: 150–51, 155

Orlando, Vittorio: 10, career, 15; in Council of Four, 16–30; reputation, 203

Outer Mongolia: 99

Overlord: 60–61, 65–68, 75

P

Palais des Nations: 144

Paris, France: meeting, December 19, 1959, 171

Paris agreements: 138, 146

Paris Peace Conference: meetings 10–

30; significance of, 194; and quiet diplomacy, 199–200

Paris Summit Conference (1960): 171–72, 177, 192; meetings, 3–4, 183–88; results of, 193; significance of, 196; timing of, 198

Pavlov, V. K.: 82

Pescadores Islands: 69

Pétain, Marshal Philippe: 27

Poincaré, Raymond: 207

Poland: 51, 77, 133–34; discussed in Council of Four, 19–20; frontiers discussed at Teheran, 62–63, 73–75; frontiers discussed at Yalta, 98–99; government in exile, 73, 81, 87, 112; Lublin government, 81, 87–88, 91–92, 94–96, 112–13; ambassadors' reports on, 96; allied quarrels over, 106–107; discussed at Potsdam, 116, 120–22, 127–28; compromise on frontiers at Potsdam, 129–30

Port Arthur, China: 99

Portugal: 68

Potsdam Summit Conference: meetings, 114–30; role of foreign ministers in, 130–31; agreements, 131, 201; results of, 131; reasons for failure, 132; Stalin's demands, 132–34; significance of, 195–96; timing of, 197–98; and quiet diplomacy, 200

Powers, Francis Gary: 4, 175ff.

Q

Quebec Conference: 55, 60

Quemoy: 139

R

Reed, John: 180

Reilly, Sir Patrick: 165

Reparations: in Council of Four, 16–17; in Yalta Conference, 85–86, 95, 97–98, 100; in Potsdam Conference, 129–30

Rhineland: 17–19, 26

Rhodes: 65
Robertson, General William: 27
Rockefeller, Nelson: 150
Rome, Treaty of: 208
Roosevelt, Elliott: 67
Roosevelt, President Franklin D.: 50, 111; career, 51; dislike of British, 51; on handling Stalin, 52; negotiations over Teheran Conference, 52–55; attitude toward Stalin, 55–56, 204; at Cairo Conference, 56–57; failure to agree with Churchill, 57; moves to Russian embassy in Teheran, 57; private meetings with Stalin at Teheran, 58–59, 63–64; at Teheran Conference, 59–75; relationship with Churchill and Stalin at Teheran, 75–77; negotiations over Yalta Conference, 80–81; in preconference discussions, 81–82; private meetings with Stalin at Yalta, 82–83, 90–91; on Germany, 83; on British policy toward France, 83; at Yalta Conference, 83–101; role in Yalta Conference, 103; goals at Yalta Conference, 105; on Stalin's policies, 106–107; death of, 107; and Congress, 201; training, 201; reputation, 203; as a planner, 207
Royal Air Force: 35
Ruhr region: 32, 130, 132
Rumania: 81, 97, 106, 119, 126–27, 131, 134
Runciman, Walter: 36
Russia: *see* Union of Soviet Socialist Republics

S

Saar region: 17–19
St. Léger, Alexis: 45
Sakhalin Island: 90–99
Scapa Flow: 28
Schmidt, Paul: 43
Spain: Stalin on, 68; discussed at Potsdam, 117

Stalin, Joseph: 39, 50, 195, 197–98; negotiations with Hitler, 50–51, 55; negotiations over Teheran Conference, 52–55, 57; private meetings with Roosevelt at Teheran, 58–59, 63–64; on De Gaulle, 59, 61, 83; at Teheran Conference, 59–75; taunts Churchill, 67, 70, 78; relationship with Roosevelt at Teheran, 76–77; aims at Teheran, 77; negotiations over Yalta Conference, 80–81; and Lublin Committee, 81; private meetings with Churchill at Yalta, 82; private meetings with Roosevelt at Yalta, 82–83, 90–91; at Yalta Conference, 83–101, 103–104; reply to Roosevelt-Churchill note on Poland, 107; meetings with Hopkins, 110–11; attitude prior to Potsdam Conference, 112; private meeting with Truman at Potsdam, 113; at Potsdam Conference, 114–30; baiting of Churchill at Potsdam, 130; failure at Potsdam, 132–34; death of, 136; and Soviet power, 201; training, 201–202; Eden on 201 n.; understanding of Roosevelt, 204
Stassen, Harold: 150
Stettin, Poland: 89
Stettinius, Edward: 81–82, 90, 94–95
Subâsič, Ivan: 117
Sudetenland: 33–34, 36–38
Suez Canal: 161
Summit Conference: evolution of, 4–8; definition of, 5–6; first proposed, 47, 207; Khrushchev's conception of, 161; proposed 1958, 165–67; criticism of, 196–97; timing of, 197; limited by time, 197–98; role of heads of government in, 198–99, 201–205; and quiet diplomacy, 199–200; and balance of power, 200–201; and the President of the United States, 205; preparation and planning, 206; uses of, 207–209; in 1914,

207; without heads of government, 208

Supreme War Council, World War I: 10

Sverdlovsk, U.S.S.R: 175–76

Swinemünde, Poland: 130

Syria: 125–33

T

Tangier: 133

Teheran Summit Conference: 55; meetings, 58–75; secret military agreement, 75; significance, 75, 77–78, 195; and quiet diplomacy, 200

Tennessee Valley Authority: 89

Test Ban Treaty: 208

Thompson, Llewellyn: 165

Tito (Josip Broz), Marshal: 60, 65, 117–18

Truman, Harry S: inexperience, 107; attitude regarding summit conference, 108–109; warned about Churchill and the British, 109; attitude toward Potsdam Conference, 111; private meeting with Churchill at Potsdam, 113; China policy, 113; private meeting with Stalin at Potsdam, 113; at Potsdam Conference, 114–30; influenced by Potsdam Conference, 196; failure in planning, 207

Truman Doctrine: 135

Turkey: 133–34; Churchill on, 60, 65, 71; Stalin on, 61, 65

Twining, General Nathan F.: 176

U

U–2 flights: 4, 8, 151, 175ff., 198, 205, 207; United States policy on, 188–92

Ukraine, U.S.S.R.: 73

Union of Soviet Socialist Republics: in Council of Four, 24; and Munich Conference, 48–49; Stalin on army, 67–68; and Far East, 69; and Cold War, 135–36; on postwar summit conference, 137; note of May 26, 1955, 140; proposed summit conference, 1958, 161–64; and U–2 flights, 177–78, 188–90

United Nations: Stalin and Roosevelt on, 63–64, 72; veto in Security Council, 86, 88; Soviet republics in, 88–89; San Francisco meetings, 91, 107, 140–41, 208; summit conference in Security Council proposed, 167–68

United States: financial aid to Europe, 22, 119; aid to U.S.S.R., 70–71; domestic politics, 72; troops in Europe, 84; State Department and Security Council, 86; Constitution, 128; State Department on summit conference, 137, 139; influence of McCarthy, 138; and tripartite note, May 10, 1955, 139–40; on foreign ministers' meeting, 164; proposal for summit conference, 1958, 165; and occupation of Berlin, 168; on Germany and summit conference, 173; State Department and U–2 flights, 178ff.; Defense Department alert, May 15, 1960, 182; and espionage, 190–92; President and summit conference, 198–99, 205

V

Versailles, Treaty of: articles 231, 25–26, 32; revision of, 26–27

Vienna, Congress of: 7

Voroshilov, Marshal K. E.: 64

W

Warsaw Pact: 146, 149

Weser River: 27–28

West Germany: 138, 143

Weygand, General Maxime: 27

White Russia: 73

White, Lincoln: 178

Wilhelm II, Kaiser: 207

Wilson, General Sir Henry: 27

Wilson, President Woodrow: 10, 197; and origins of Council of Four, 11–12; career and character of, 15–16; in Council of Four, 16–30; personal negotiations, 198–99; and Congress, 201; personality and negotiations, 202; reputation of, 203; failure to plan, 206

World War I: 7–11, 67

Y

Yagushkin, Sergeant V.: 178

Yalta Agreements: 99–100, 106–107, 115, 118, 133, 140, 201

Yalta Conference: negotiations over, 80–81; size of delegations, 82; meetings, 83–101; Far Eastern Agreement, 99–100; significance, 101–102, 105, 195; timing of, 197–98; and quiet diplomacy, 200

Young, George: 153

Yugoslavia: 75, 81; discussed at Potsdam, 117–18

Z

Zhukov, Marshal G. K.: 146–47, 153

The text of *The Summit Conferences, 1919–1960* has been set on the Linotype in 11-point Caledonia, a type designed by the late W. A. Dwiggins, the eminent American graphic artist. The paper on which this volume is printed bears the University of Oklahoma Press watermark and has an effective life of at least three hundred years.